Dream*Makers

Crayola

Visual Arts & Social Studies

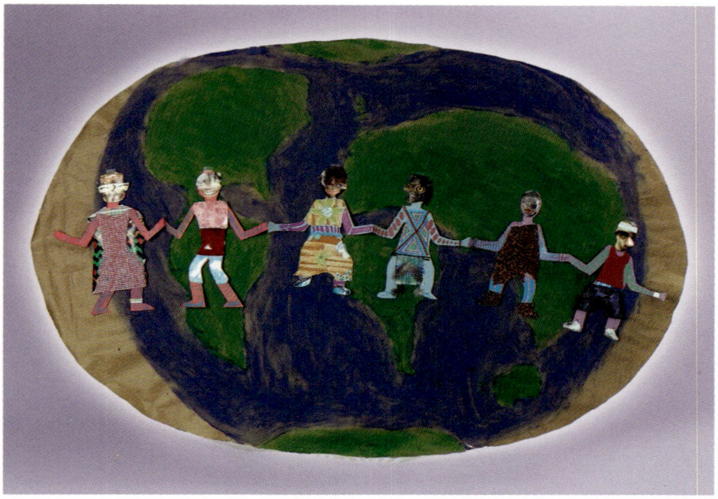

DREAMS THAT SUPPORT A CHANGING WORLD

Twelve Standards-Based Lessons
for Classroom and Art Teachers K-6

16th Edition

BINNEY & SMITH A Hallmark Company
Easton, Pennsylvania

Credits

Director of School and Organized Activities
Nancy DeBellis

For Crayola® Dream-Makers® 16, Dreams That Support a Changing World Managing Editor
Ron DeLong

Authors
Ron DeLong
Abbie Lezak

Editors
Donna Chastain
Janet Brown McCracken

Photographer
Peter M. Sak

Editorial Assistance by
Tavy Thomas

For Crayola.com Dream-Makers Resources
Jacqualyne M. Flynn

Binney & Smith gratefully acknowledges the teachers who tested the lessons in this guide:
Barbi Bailey-Smith, Little River Elementary School, Durham, North Carolina
Billie Capps, Little River Elementary School, Durham, North Carolina
Judi Collier, Little River Elementary School, Durham, North Carolina
Trish Davlantes, Jordan Community School, Chicago, Illinois
Marcia Effinger, Brenham Independent School District, Brenham, Texas
Pam Gall, Maple Avenue Middle School, Littlestown, Pennsylvania
Pam Leister, Jordan Community School, Chicago, Illinois
Abbie Lezak, Saucon Valley Middle School, Bethlehem, PA
Elyse Martin, Jordan Community School, Chicago, Illinois
Judy Mazzucco, Millstone Township Elementary School, Clarksburg, New Jersey
Jen O'Flaherty, Sandy Plains Elementary School, Baltimore, Maryland
Jennifer Parks, T.J. Lee Elementary School, Irving, Texas
Neila Steiner, C.S. 102, Bronx, New York
Bobbi Yancey, College Oaks Elementary School, Lake Charles, Louisiana
Sandy Young, Williamsport Elementary School, Williamsport, Pennsylvania
Marilyn Zoller Koral, Everett Middle School, San Francisco, California

Additional thanks for their assistance and support to:
Mike Charles
Barbara Benton
Lynn Berkowitz, Ringling Museum of Art, Sarasota, Florida
Jill Jamison
Justin Knecht
Charles McAnall
Cheri Sterman
Heidi Taylor, Ringling Museum of Art, Sarasota, Florida
Michelle Wollman
Eric Zebley

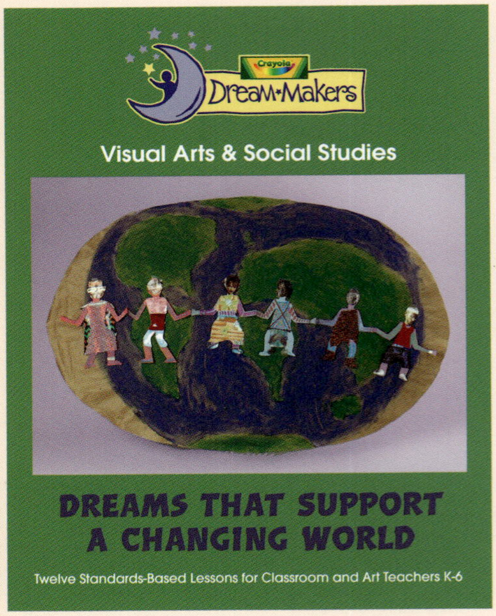

Front Cover:
Photograph by Peter M Sak, Student artwork by students from CS 102 Bronx, New York. Teacher: Neila Steiner

Design:
First Generation, Allentown, PA

Printed in the United States of America

ISBN: 0-86696-319-7

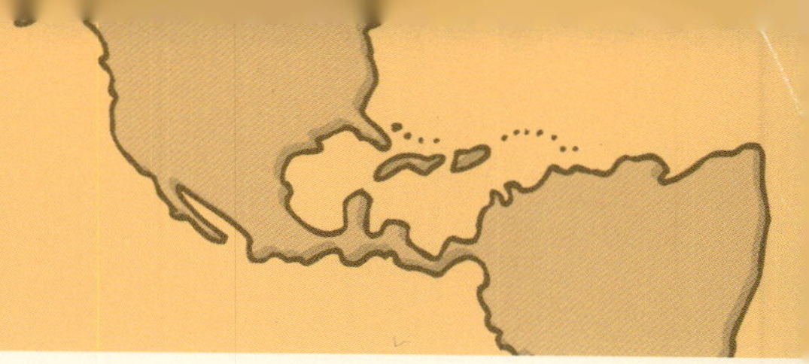

Table of Contents

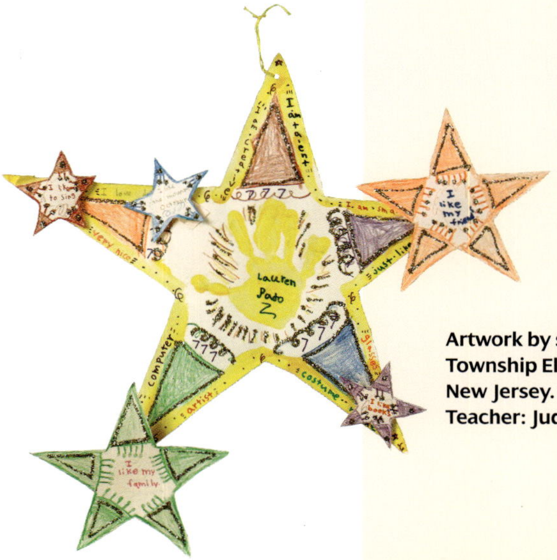

Artwork by students from Millstone Township Elementary School, Clarksburg, New Jersey.
Teacher: Judy Mazzucco

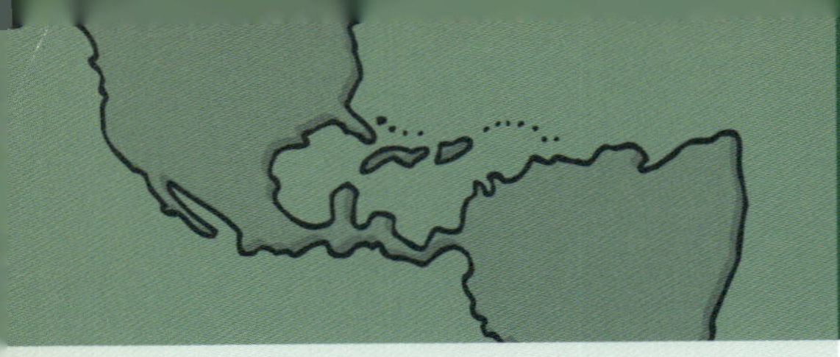

Introduction

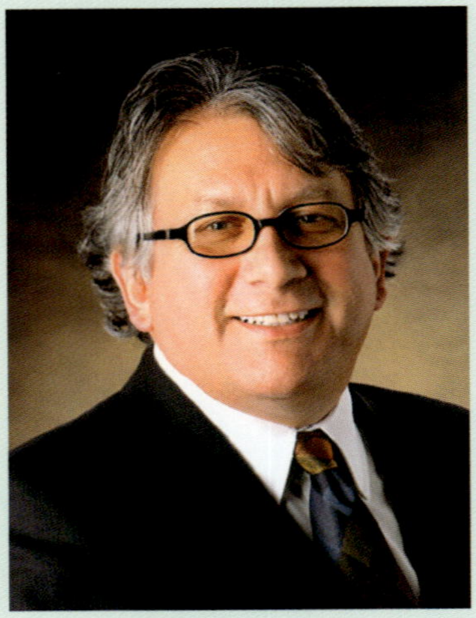

The Crayola Dream-Makers Teachers Resource Guide – Visual Arts and Social Studies – Building Dreams That Support A Changing World is a curriculum resource designed for both art and classroom teachers. The guide contains 12 standards-based lessons that focus on real-life, hands-on activities that help children comprehend their relationship to the society in which they live. At the same time it provides teachers with the instructional steps needed to teach students the habits of creative social behavior.

Engaging students in the study of social behavior through the visual arts helps them develop a deeper understanding of Social Studies that will benefit them throughout their lives.

This guide specifically examines people and the behaviors, characteristics and interactions that define their culture and civilization, particularly as expressed by the development and use of written languages and advances in the arts, the sciences and government. Artifacts of civilizations that are sacredly housed in museums worldwide are a reflection of these people's dreams, social interactions and results of their changes to build better world.

Consider this:

- Today's advanced technologies developed by creative minds permit us to see cartographic images that were not available to early civilizations. A map from the 14th century reveals shapes and lines that differ dramatically from today's satellite maps.
- A Umntwana Doll, designed by South African artist Corlia de Bruyn is dramatically different from a Initiatio Doll adorned in beadwork, felt and metal, and different still from an American Indian Apache Doll. These visual differences in dolls allow children to visually compare and contrast beliefs, customs and behaviors from different cultures.
- The design reflected in Thomas Hart Benton's painting, Interior Space, demonstrates a perspective of early 20th century home design that students today can see in their own bedrooms.

Renowned educator Elliot Eisner said "the arts teach children that problems can have more than one solution. The arts teach children that in complex forms of problem solving, purposes are seldom fixed, but change with circumstance and opportunity. Learning in the arts requires the ability and a willingness to surrender to the unanticipated possibilities of the work as it unfolds."

As you apply this curriculum resource in your instruction it will help your students view their world much differently.

- Think about the impact on student learning when you challenge them to create campaign posters that highlight positive civil attributes of a classmate they endorse as a candidate for "Community Leader."
- Consider what students will realize when they investigate doll adornments from other cultures and then design "We are the Children" paper dolls that reflect a civilization's values, beliefs and achievements reflective of the art of Romare Bearden.
- Imagine how you will impact your students' learning when they hear your presentation on Martin Luther King's "I Have A Dream" speech and then develop a 3-dimensional historical time-line that portrays this civil rights issue.

Through our dreams, we can change the world. Take some time to explore these and all the lessons in this guide that will expand you and your student's ability to creatively dream. Imagine what civilizations thousands of years from now will learn about society today if we continue to build and create social societies that are rich through their visual arts.

– Ron DeLong

Source: *Learning and the Arts: Crossing Boundaries* Proceedings from an invitational meeting for education, arts and youth funders held January 12-14, 2000, Los Angeles Organized by Geraldine R. Dodge Foundation, J. Paul Getty Trust, and The John D. and Catherine T. Mac Arthur Foundation

Alliances, Collaborations, and Exhibition

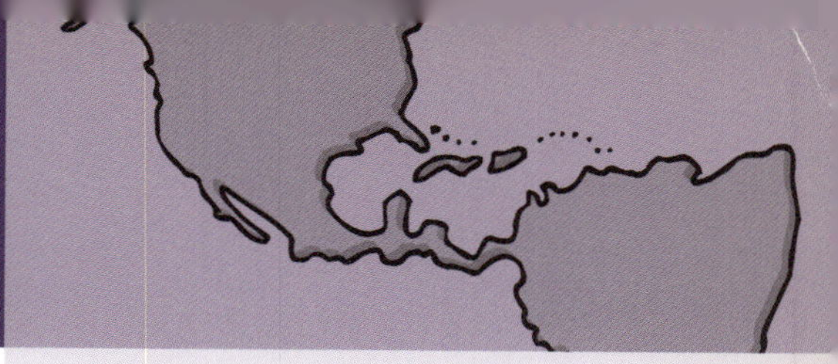

Collaboration Works!

Understanding that collaboration is a key to success in schools, we developed the lessons in this guide to encourage and support collaborative work. Although individual teachers can easily present lessons, we have broken out preparation steps and discussion starters to simplify teamwork and/or peer consultation. Of course, teachers benefit when tasks are shared, but students also benefit when they see more than one adult supporting their efforts.

Besides fellow art or classroom teachers, any of the following could have a place on your team: new teachers, reading specialists, librarians, parents, artists, art groups, and local art agencies.

Here are some steps for a successful team process. This can work whether you are jointly presenting a lesson over a few class periods or putting on a school- or community-wide exhibition.

1. First, share this guide with your collaborators before your first meeting, so they have an idea of what to expect.
2. Meet to agree on your goals and develop an action plan. Identify the steps you need to take and decide who will be responsible for each.
3. Make a calendar that includes the important milestones and allows adequate time for each process.
4. Work your plan. Have periodic meetings or phone calls to make sure you keep on track.
5. Don't forget to celebrate your success and recognize everyone who lent support. If you are presenting an exhibition, use the Dream-Makers "helpers" certificate (which you can download from Crayola.com/dreammakers) or make your own.
6. Assess results. What are your "lessons learned"?

Planning Your Own Exhibition

Publicly exhibiting their art is one of the most exciting and rewarding gifts you can give your students. Having an exhibition opening is a wonderful way to engage the school, parents, and community, especially if members of different groups help plan and put on the event. Here are some suggestions for a successful experience:

- Always display all students' work that was generated by the Dream-Makers activities.
- Exhibit artwork in a way that honors the students.
- Matting the artwork can be simple and inexpensive. For ideas on mounting and exhibiting artwork, go to Crayola.com/successguide, and click on the Art Teacher Guide.
- Consider displaying the student's dream statements along with the work. These can be especially compelling for adults viewing the work.
- You can demonstrate the value of your program by displaying the standards the lesson addressed with the artwork.
- If you select art to submit to the national program, develop selection criteria based on your school's or district's guidelines for assessment.

For your opening, enlist the help of parents and local businesses. Serve child-friendly refreshments and have a simple ceremony/photo op for presenting certificates of recognition to students and helpers. Invite district and community leaders so you can showcase their support.

YOUR COMMUNITY: Bridges Toward Creative Collaboration, a Crayola® "Strategies for Success" Guide

As advocates for the arts, we've worked with many community organizations, large and small, across the country. Over the years we've found that some are more successful than others at sustaining community support and engagement. One of the best we've known is the Kennedy Center Imagination Celebration (KCIC) in Colorado Springs, Colorado. We recently asked them to share their experience in using the arts to engage people to build and sustain a creative community. The result is a twelve-page guide to thinking big, starting small, and working collaboratively toward cultural connections. Topics covered include:

- Create a team with vision and mission
- Construct a strategic plan
- Identify resources in your community
- Build relationships and support collaborations
- Create vibrant, inclusive, and economically sound events
- Recognize and celebrate collaborators
- Sustain your success

For more information, including a free downloadable pdf, go to Crayola.com/successguide and click on the Community Success Guide.

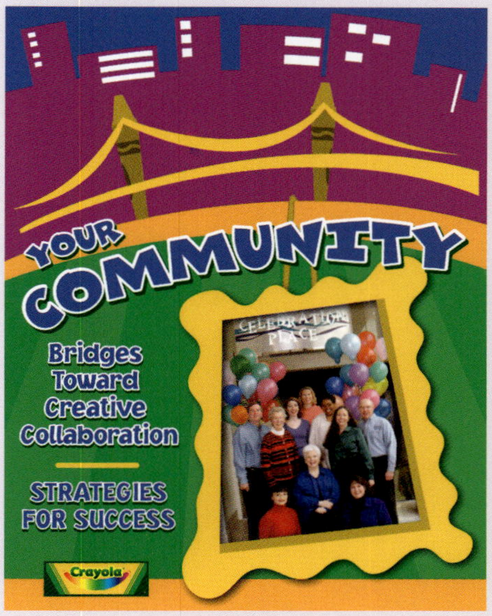

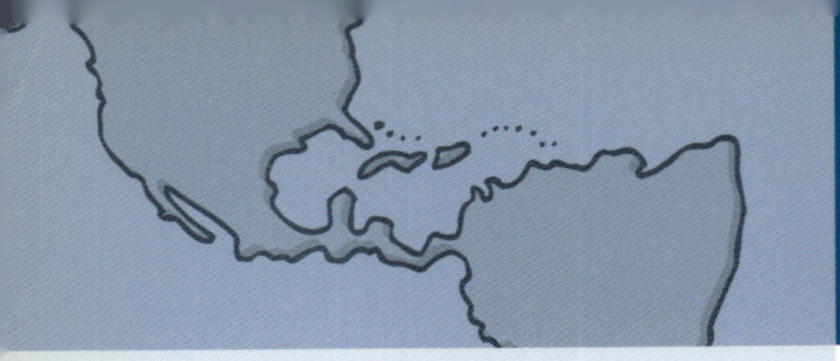

About Crayola® Dream-Makers®

Social Studies in Art History

The entire body of Art History is virtually a visual textbook of Social Studies. Works of art from the past show us how, where, and with whom people lived, loved, warred, and carried out their daily lives. They show us—in ways that range from the documentary to the highly idealized—what people truly were as well as how they wished they could be, or be seen.

Beyond representing people and situations from their own experience or imaginations, visual artists have also brought home images of the richness and strangeness of other lands and cultures. These ethnographic illustrations reveal social attitudes that range from respect, as seen in meticulous idealized images, to prejudice and fear, as seen in a fascination with grotesque or frightening depictions.

A whole genre of painting from the Spanish colonies in the Americas revolved around the physical and cultural differences seen or imagined in people born of mixed race. The purpose of these "casta," or caste, paintings was not just to show interesting images, but also to illustrate an elaborate and rigid class structure. As historical documents, they reveal as much about the artists and the patrons who commissioned them as they do about the people they portray.

Crayola Dream-Makers is a national program that encourages the creative development and learning of children in Kindergarden through 6th grade, recognizes student artists, and displays children's artwork in a national exhibition. Since 1984, millions of students and thousands of art and classroom teachers have participated in the program. Dream-Makers has been recognized by the U.S. Department of Education, the John F. Kennedy Center for the Performing Arts, the National Association of Elementary School Principals, the Association of Children's Museums, the National Art Education Association, and other leading arts and education organizations.

Since its inception, the program has collected 3,300 works of art by children, which are professionally framed and matted, documented, used as teaching tools, and exhibited to advocate art education. A large part of the collection decorates the offices of the U.S. Department of Education in Washington, D.C. To view children's artwork from past years of the program, log on to Crayola.com/dreammakers and visit the Gallery of Children's Art.

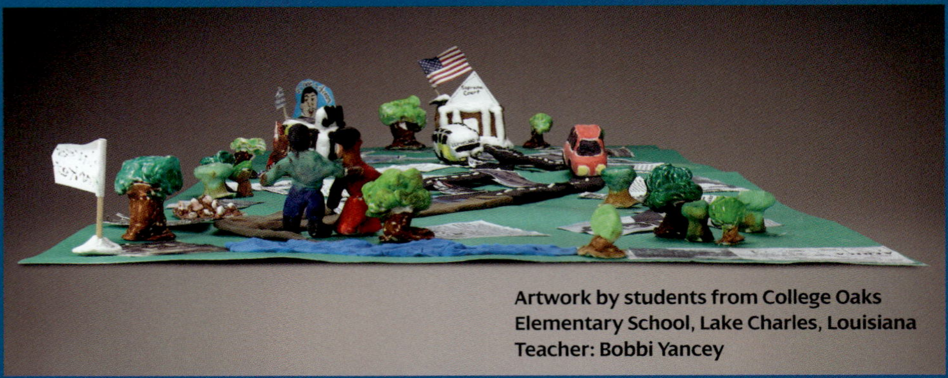

Artwork by students from College Oaks Elementary School, Lake Charles, Louisiana
Teacher: Bobbi Yancey

Mastering Social Studies Concepts Through Visual Art

Working in a group on a Dream-Makers lesson can lead to a deeper understanding of our shared history and a greater enthusiasm for the subject. Bobbi Yancey of College Oaks Elementary School, Lake Charles, Louisiana, found this when she tested *Rosa Takes a Freedom Ride* with her class:

"We wanted the project to be authentic, so we used information and pictures from the Internet and books, and did our own drawing for some things. We found the Jacob Lawrence 'Migration Series' and felt that his series 'spoke' to what we were trying to show in our timeline, so we incorporated reproductions of his paintings. My students' personal experience, coupled with their research and 'I can't believe they did that' comments, kept them excited, inspired, and creative."

The results of this intense collaboration illustrate the lesson on pages 30-31.

Funding Your Program

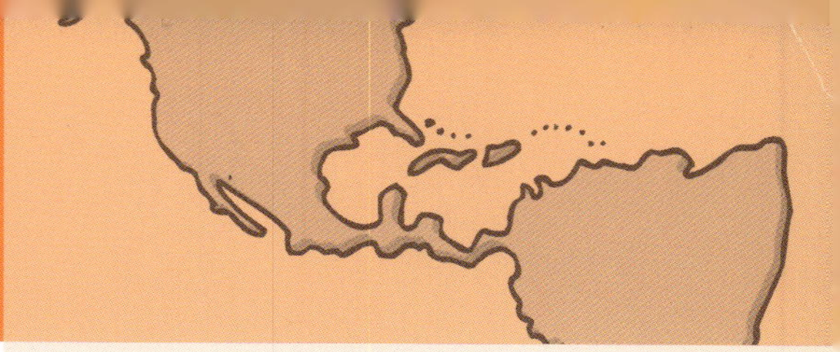

Ways of Funding a Dream-Makers Program

Funding your program is always a challenge. The process of prospecting for funds is grounded in the conviction that a partnership should develop between the community seeking funds and the organization that provides the funds. Dollars have no value until they are attached to solid programs. Bringing organizations together effectively can result in dynamic collaborations.

Funding takes time and persistence, and a good solution is to follow a step-by-step process in the search for dollars to fund your project or your program in your community.

Raising funds is definitely an investment in the future of your program, your school and your community. Your aim should be to build a network of organizations that can help on a steady basis.

The recommended process is not a formula to be adhered to rigidly. We suggest that you approach the process keeping in mind the specific needs of your program, your school, and your community. Always be creative and remember the words of educational guru Madeline Hunter, "Modify and adjust."

Gather Your Proposal Information

Your proposal will require documentation in three areas: concept, program, and expenses. Pull together a team to help gather information. The data gathering process makes the actual writing much easier. Involving others in the project helps others understand the value of the project to your organization.

Adopt a Compelling Concept

Make sure the project fits into the mission and the philosophy of your organization. Funders want to know that a project reinforces the overall direction of an organization, and they may need to be convinced that the case for the project is compelling.

Detail Your Program

When making requests, consider the information that potential sponsors will need:

- The nature of the program and how it will be conducted
- The timetable for the program
- The anticipated outcomes and how best to evaluate the results
- Staffing and volunteer needs

Detail Expenses

Don't pin down all the expenses connected to the project until the program details and timing have been worked out. Financial gathering takes place after the narrative part of the master proposal has been written. Consider maintaining outlines of needs at this point.

Components of a Proposal

Executive Summary: Umbrella statement of your case and summary of the entire proposal – 1 page
Statement of Need: Why this project is necessary – 2 pages
Project Description: Nuts and bolts of how the project will be implemented and evaluated – 3 pages
Budget: Financial description of the project plus explanatory notes – 1 page
Organization Information: History and governing structure of the nonprofit; its primary activities, audiences, and services – 1 page
Conclusion: Summary of the proposal's main points – 2 paragraphs

For more information about grants and grant writing visit *The Foundation Center* at www.fdncenter.org.

Dream-Makers on the Web

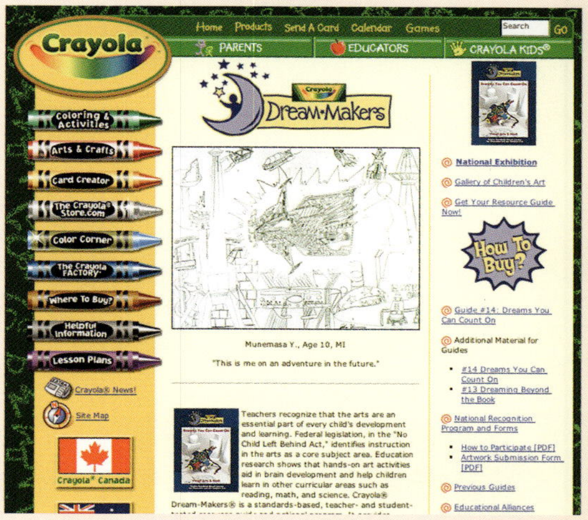

Crayola.com/dreammakers includes extensive supplementary material for the program and the guide. Features include:

- Additional material for each lesson – extensions, adaptations, content webs, and links to resources
- Content from past Dream-Makers guides
- Printable certificates for recognizing children's participation and adult's support
- Thousands of images of children's Dream-Makers art from the last 20 years
- How to order guides
- And much more!

Consider developing your own curriculum links, aligned with your school board-approved curricula. Your district Curriculum Coordinator or Supervisor can help you align lessons with your school's educational goals.

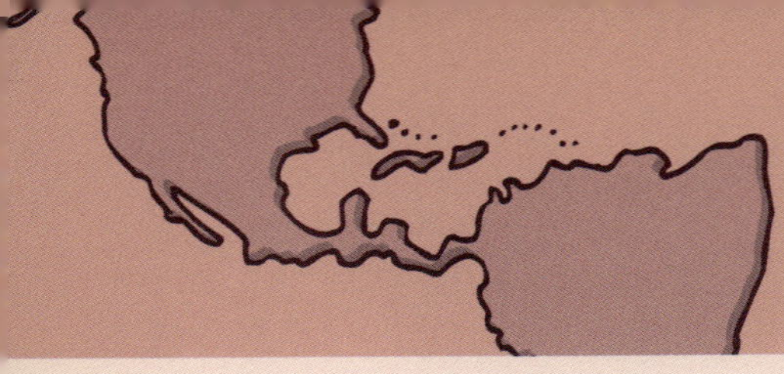

National Visual Arts Standards

Below are Content Standards from the voluntary National Visual Arts Standards, and a brief synopsis of the corresponding Achievement Standards. Although many educators are well acquainted with these, they are included here for easy reference. While these standards have not been adopted in full by each state, most state standards correspond with or are based on National Standards.

For information about the complete standards book, which includes a useful introduction and rationale for each age group, call the National Art Education Association at 1-800-299-8321, or visit their website at www.naea-reston.org.

Content Standards	Achievement Standards Synopsis for Grades K-4 & 5-8	
1. Understanding and applying media, techniques, and processes	In K-4, students recognize various materials, techniques and processes, and can describe and use these to communicate ideas, experiences, and stories, and to elicit viewer response. In K-8, students use materials and tools safely.	In 5-8, students select media, techniques and processes to enhance communication, then analyze whether or not these choices were effective, and reflect on the reasons.
2. Using knowledge of structures and functions	In K-4, students recognize different ways visual characteristics, expressive features and organizational principles communicate ideas and elicit different responses.	In 5-8, students generalize about the effects of visual structures and functions of art, use these to improve their own work's communication potential, and reflect upon whether or not these uses were effective.
3. Choosing and evaluating a range of subject matter, symbols and ideas	In K-4, students explore and understand prospective content for their art, then select and use appropriate subjects, symbols and ideas to make art meaningful.	In 5-8, students integrate concepts with content to communicate intended meaning as they work, using subjects, themes, and symbols that demonstrate knowledge of their work's contexts, values and aesthetics.
4. Understanding the visual arts in relation to history and cultures	In K-4, students understand that visual arts and specific artworks have a history and identifiable relationship to various cultures, times and places, and that time, place, culture and art influence each other.	In 5-8, students identify, describe, and compare characteristics of select artworks from various eras and cultures; identify the work's places along a cultural timeline; relate how time/place influence a work's visual characteristics.
5. Reflecting upon and assessing the characteristics and merits of their work and the work of others	In K-4, students understand/describe purposes for creating artworks, how people's experiences influence a work, how various viewer's responses to one work differ.	In 5-8, students compare purposes for creating works; analyze a specific work's meaning by reviewing its history/culture; describe and compare responses to their own artworks and responses to works of other eras/cultures.
6. Making connections between visual arts and other disciplines	In K-4, students understand/use similarities and differences between visual arts and other arts disciplines. They find connections between visual arts and other subjects.	In 5-8, students compare characteristics of works in two or more art forms that share similar subject matter, eras, or cultural context. They describe the interrelationships between art and the principles/subject matter of other disciplines.

To learn more about art education's impact on children's development and learning, the Arts Education Partnership has published the following resources:

- *Critical Links: Learning in the Arts and Student Academic and Social Development (2002).* This compendium summarizes and discusses 62 research studies that examine the effects of arts learning on students' social and academic skills.
- *Champions of Change: The Impact of the Arts on Learning (1999).* This report compiles seven major studies that provide evidence of enhanced learning and achievement when students are involved in a variety of arts experiences.

These resources are available on the Arts Education Partnership's website at www.aep-arts.org.

National Social Studies Standards

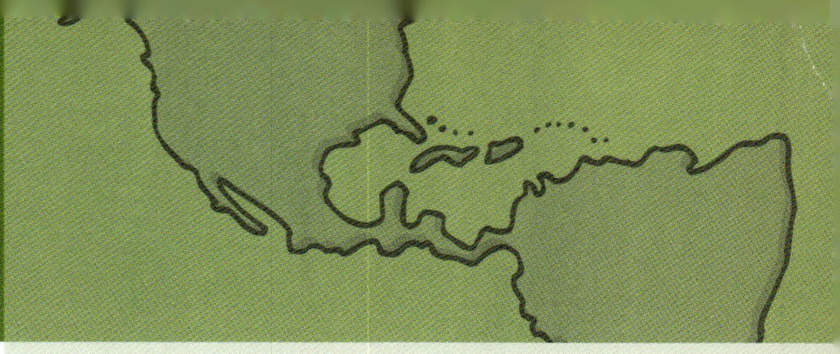

Ten Social Studies Thematic Strands that form the basis of the Social Studies Standards

1. **Culture – experiences that provide for the study of culture and cultural diversity.**
   - Give examples of how experiences may be interpreted differently by people from diverse cultural perspectives and frames of reference.
   - Describe ways in which language, stories, folktales, music and artistic creations serve as expressions of culture and influence behavior of people living in a particular culture.

2. **Time, Continuity, and Change – experiences that provide for the study of the ways human beings view themselves in and over time.**
   - Demonstrate an understanding that different people may describe the same event or situation in diverse ways, citing reasons for the differences in views.

3. **People, Places, and Environments – experiences that provide for the study of people, place and environments.**
   - Use appropriate resources, data sources, and geographic tools such as atlases, data bases, grid systems, charts, graphs, and maps to generate, manipulate, and interpret information.
   - Describe how people create places that reflect ideas, personality, culture, and wants and needs as they design homes, playgrounds, classrooms, and the like.

4. **Individual Development and Identity – experiences that provide for the study of individual development and identity.**
   - Describe the unique features of one's nuclear and extended families.

5. **Individuals, Groups, and Institutions – experiences that provide for the study of interactions among individuals, groups, and institutions.**
   - Identify roles as learned behavior patterns in group situations such as student, family members, peer play group member, or club member.

6. **Power, Authority, and Governance – experiences that provide for the study of how people create and change structures of power, authority, and governance.**
   - Examine the rights and responsibilities of the individual in relation to his or her social group, such as family, peer group, and school class.

7. **Production, Distribution, and Consumption – experiences that provide for the study of how people organize for the production, distribution and consumption of goods and services.**
   - Describe how we depend upon workers with specialized jobs and the ways in which they contribute to the production and exchange of goods and services.

8. **Science, Technology, and Society – experiences that provide for the study of relationships among science, technology, and society.**
   - Suggest ways to monitor science and technology in order to protect the physical environment, individual rights, and the common good.

9. **Global Connections – experiences that provide for the study of global connections and interdependence.**
   - Explore ways that language, art, music, belief systems, and other cultural elements may facilitate global understanding or lead to misunderstanding;
   - Give examples of conflict, cooperation, and interdependence among individuals, groups and nations.

10. **Civic Ideals and Practices – experiences that provide for the study of the ideals, principles, and practices of citizenship in a democratic republic, so that the learner can:**
    - Recognize and interpret how the "common good" can be strengthened through various forms of citizen action.

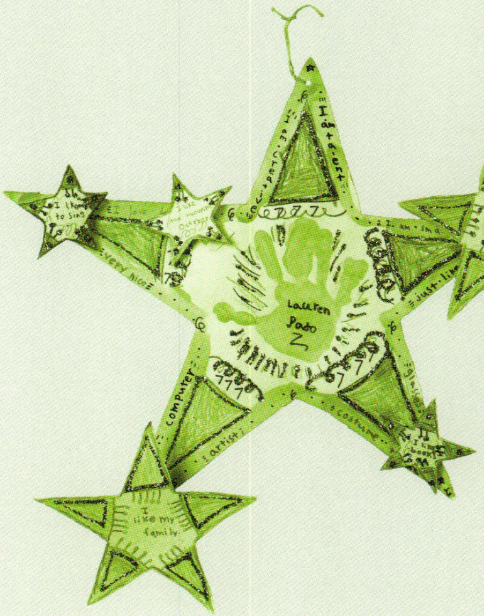

Note: Because of space limitations, we have included only the particular standards under each thematic strand that are referenced by lessons in this guide. For the full standards under each strand, see the complete work, Expectations of Excellence: Curriculum Standards for Social Studies, published by the National Council for the Social Studies. More information is available at www.socialstudies.org or by calling (800) 683-0812.

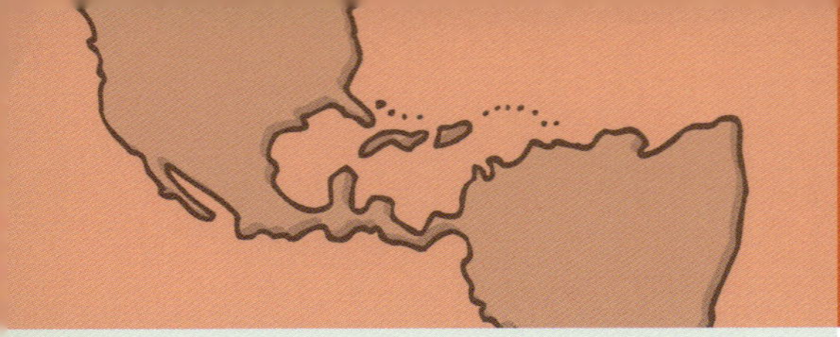

A Forest of Family Trees

Grade Level
K-2

Classroom Time
Two to three 40-min. periods

Materials/Tools

- Cardboard or oak tag
- Cardboard tubes or 8" x 11" oak tag
- Chenille stems (brown)
- Coffee filters (optional)
- Construction paper (green)
- Crayola® Construction Paper™ Crayons
- Crayola Model Magic®
- Crayola School Glue
- Crayola Scissors
- Crayola Washable Markers
- Hole punch (optional)

Tips
Ask families to recycle cardboard tubes from gift wrap, plastic wrap, and paper towels.

Resources
Celebrating Families by Rosamarie Hausherr
Climbing Your Family Tree: Online and Off-line Genealogy for Kids by Ira Wolfman
Home Is Where Your Family Is by Katie Kavanagh
Me and My Family Tree by Joan Sweeney
Who's Who in My Family? by Loreen Leedy

Visual Arts Standard 2
Using knowledge of structure and functions.

Social Studies Standard IV
Individual Development and Identity

Objective

Students create family tree sculptures that illustrate the unique features of their families and then become part of a class forest.

Teacher Preparation

Classroom Teacher: Read *Who's Who in My Family?* or a similar book. Explain what nuclear and extended families are. Talk about the families that children know. Discuss the interests, beliefs, ideas, and traditions that families share. How are families influenced by where they live?

Art Teacher: Display pictures of trees from all over the world, especially those in various climates. Create one family tree as an example. Prepare tree parts to demonstrate one way to assemble a tree.

Discussion Starters

Classroom Teacher: "Think about your family. Is your family like your friends families?" Discuss how they are alike/different. Create a list of things that their families share, think are important, are interested in, and have in common. Brainstorm words: mom, dad, brother, sister, love, truth, movies, hiking, baseball, vacation, working hard,... Use pictures from magazines or symbols such as hearts to inspire thinking.

Art Teacher: Look at the pictures of trees and discuss differences and similarities. "Think of the trees that grow in our area. Are they short or tall? Do they have long branches? Thick trunks? Think about these features when creating your family tree."

Process

Form Tree Trunk and Base

1. Cut one end of a cardboard tube into half-inch strips (rolled and glued oak tag can also be used).
2. Decorate the trunk with Construction Paper Crayons or washable markers.
3. Cut a 6-inch circle from cardboard or oak tag. Decorate this base with Construction Paper Crayons. Glue strips on the bottom of the trunk to base. Anchor the tree trunk by surrounding the base with Model Magic.

Bend Branches

1. Wrap a chenille stem or rubber band around the base of a bunch of 8 to 10 chenille stems to hold them together.
2. Place chenille stems into the tree trunk, leaving about 2/3 of the stem outside the trunk.
3. Bend the chenille stems to resemble branches.

Design Leaves

1. Cut leaves or other shapes from construction paper and fold in half.
2. Write family members' names, interests, and/or values on the leaves with Construction Paper Crayons. Draw family symbols and pictures on the leaves. Color the leaves.
3. Punch two holes in leaves and thread chenille stems through them for branches.
4. Display all family trees to create a forest.

Assessment

Summarize learning. Ask students to describe the unique features of their families to the class.

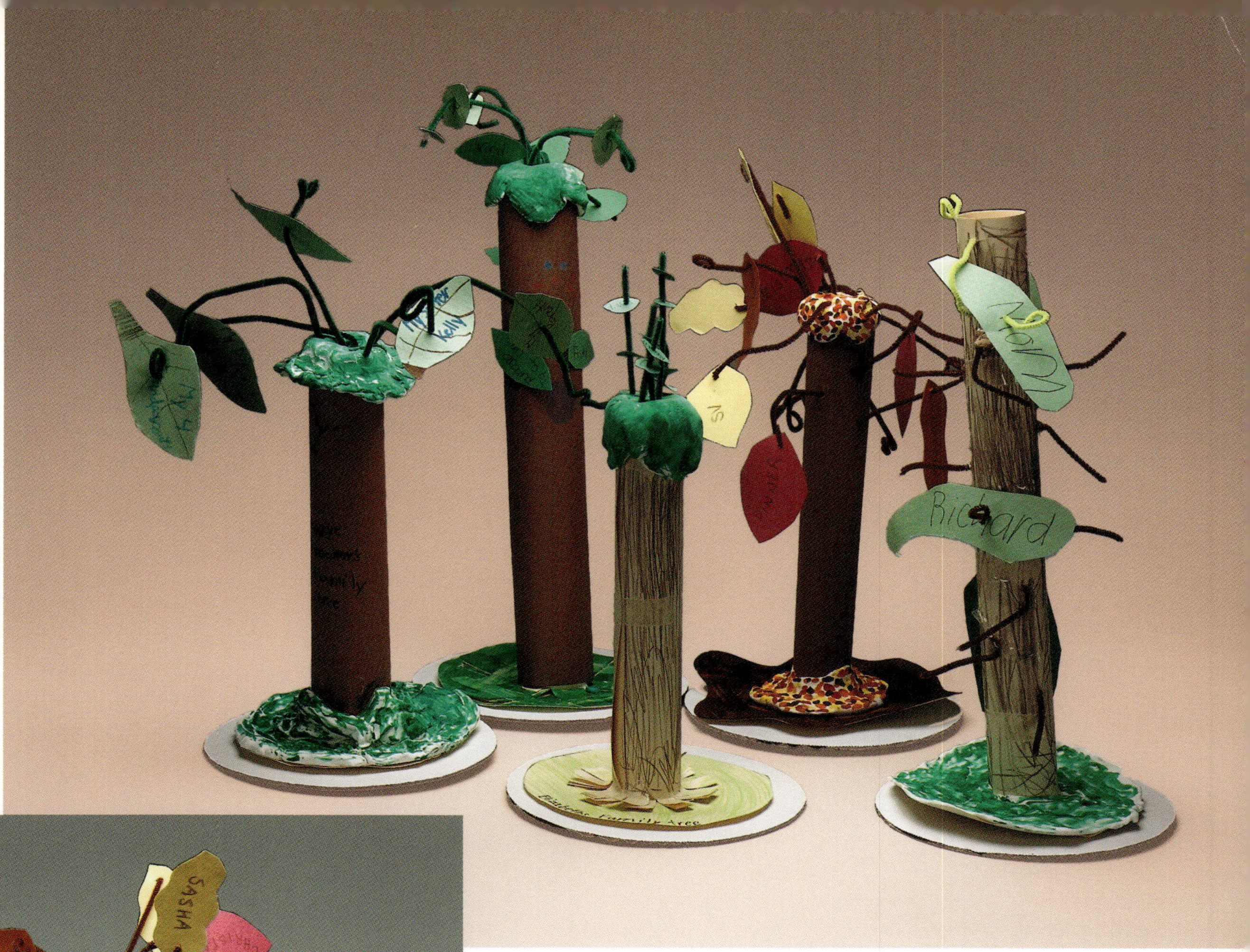

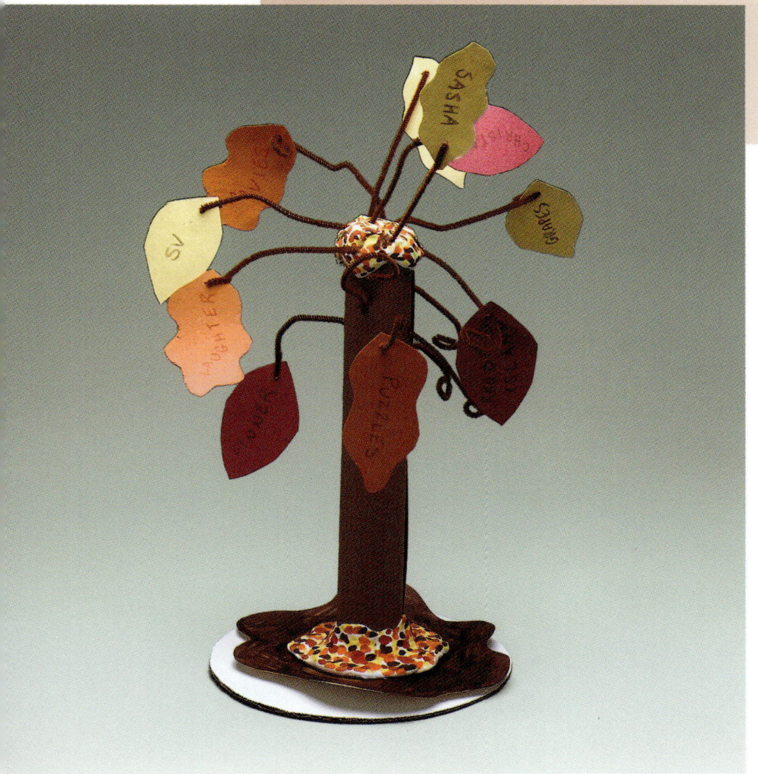

Artwork by students from Saucon Valley Elementary School, Hellertown, Pennsylvania. Teacher: Mrs. Stephanie Laudenslager

Background Information

During the Victorian Era, making decorative family trees became a popular pastime. Family trees were used as wall hangings and were elaborately decorated with angels, wreaths, banners, and pictures of family members. The trend became increasingly popular as printers starting selling black and white lithographs that were later painted by the owner. Bibles contained smaller versions of family trees. Magazines printed tear-out versions. Many women made embroidered and quilted versions. Recording family history has become a science that requires much research and record keeping.

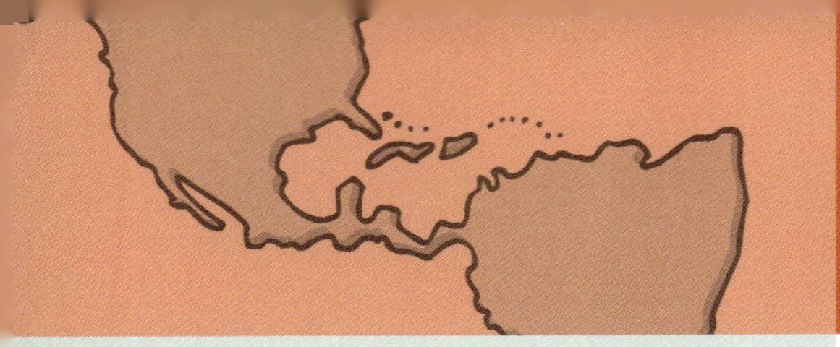

Classroom Stars of Fame

Grade Level
K-2

Classroom Time
Two 40-min. periods

Materials/Tools
- Crayola® Fingerpaint (yellow)
- Crayola Glitter Glue
- Crayola Glue Sticks
- Crayola Scissors
- Crayola So Big® Crayons
- Oak tag
- Recycled newspaper

Tips
Cover your painting area with newspaper.
Keep painted stars from curling by using heavier paper such as oak tag or corrugated cardboard, or paint both sides of lightweight papers.

Resources
Girl, You're Amazing! by Virginia Kroll
The Upside Down Boy/El Niño de Cabeza by Juan Felipe Herrera
Three Cheers for Tacky by Helen Lester

Visual Arts Standard 1
Understanding and applying media, techniques, and processes.

Social Studies Standard V
Individuals, Groups, and Institutions

Objective
Students learn how every individual is unique by creating stars that symbolize the roles they play in the lives of others.

Teacher Preparation
Classroom Teacher: Read children's books that focus on roles such as family member, student, friend, or club or team member. Research the Hollywood Walk of Fame on Hollywood Boulevard and display photos.

Art Teacher: Create a path of large and small painted stars on a wall. Research, collect, cut out, and display signs and symbols that reflect personal attributes and roles.

Discussion Starters
Classroom Teacher: Start a discussion around the roles people fill in life. Brainstorm what some of the students' roles are. "Do your roles ever change? Can you be more than one role at a time? What roles do you like the best?"

Art Teacher: Stars in the Hollywood Walk of Fame are decorated with one of five symbols: movie camera, record, microphone, radio, or theatrical masks. How can you design your stars so that they represent your roles? What colors, shapes, and textures will convey your roles clearly?

Process
Create a Large Background Star

1 Draw a large star on oak tag. Cut it out. Fingerpaint the star yellow. Air-dry the paint.
2. Use crayons to fill the star with words and symbols that describe you. Show your dreams for the future, too.

Make Small Role Stars

1. Cut out one small star for each role you have. Make stars for parents, friends, and siblings if you wish.
2. Using glitter glue and crayons, decorate the stars with symbols and colors representing roles.
3. Cut strips of oak tag. Accordion-fold the strips. Use the strips to glue small stars to large stars. Display the stars in a large space.

Assessment
Ask students to study their classmates' stars. Which stars best match the students who created them?

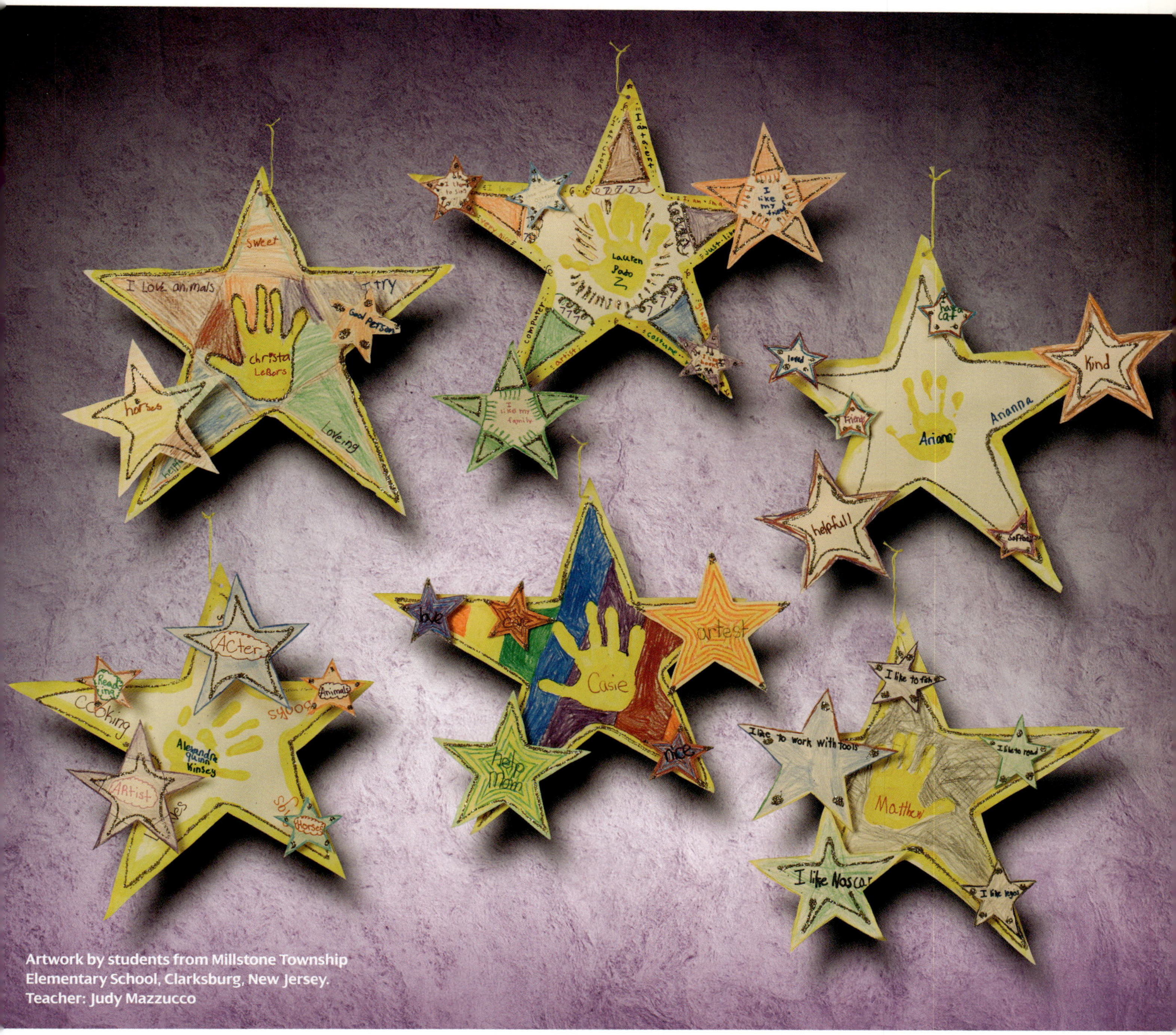

Artwork by students from Millstone Township Elementary School, Clarksburg, New Jersey. Teacher: Judy Mazzucco

Background Information

The Hollywood Walk of Fame is the world's most famous sidewalk. Its five acres of terrazzo and brass stars are recognized worldwide as a tribute to some of Hollywood's greatest contributors. Each star includes the honoree's name and an emblem representing motion pictures, television, radio, recording, or live theatre. One person could be honored in each category for a total of five Walk of Fame stars! The first presentation ceremony was held on February 9, 1960. Every month, one or two new honorees receive stars at a cost of $15,000 per ceremony. More than 2,000 artists have been honored on the Walk of Fame.

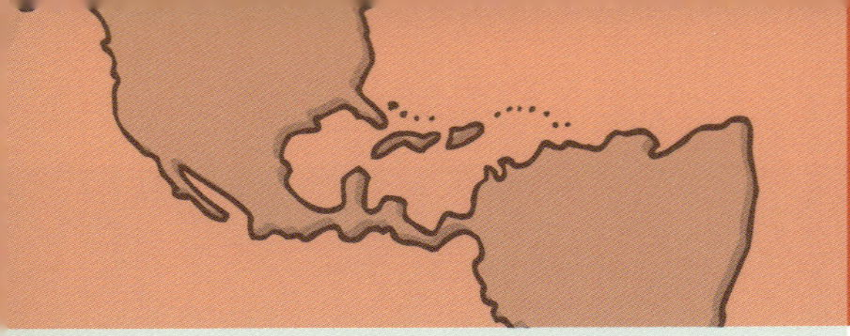

Designing Diversity Dolls

Grade Level
K-2

Classroom Time
Two 40-min. periods

Materials/Tools
- Crayola® Model Magic® (assorted colors)
- Crayola Paint Brushes
- Crayola School Glue
- Crayola Watercolor Colored Pencils
- Crayola Watercolors
- Paper towels
- Recycled newspaper
- Water containers

Tips
Toy catalogs and children's books are good visual resources for doll images. Protect your painting area with newspaper. Air-dry dolls before applying watercolor pencil or paint to achieve hard-edged design effects. Gently dab glue over dried watercolor to create a glaze over the doll.

Resources
The Art of the Russian Matryoshka by Rett Ertl, Rick Hibbard, and Yakov Chitov
The Littlest Matryoshka by Corine Demas Bliss
The Magic Nesting Doll by Jacqueline K. Ogburn and Laurel Long

Visual Arts Standard 2
Understanding the visual arts in relation to history and culture.

Social Studies Standards I
Culture

Objective
Students create and compare characteristics observed in doll designs from different cultures.

Teacher Preparation
Classroom Teacher: Display pictures or replicas of various types of dolls reflective of an assortment of world cultures.

Art Teacher: Display miniature dolls that illustrate characteristics observed in various cultures. Point out simple three-dimensional forms observed in the doll-like forms, such as spheres, cylinders, rectangles, and cubes, that become the basis for more complex doll designing.

Discussion Starters
Classroom Teacher: Share images of dolls with the class. Discuss differences observed in designs of dolls from various cultures. Discuss how doll designers include specific objects when they make dolls, so the doll reflects a particular culture. Talk about the clothing and how it differs from culture to culture.

Art Teacher: Ask students to bring dolls to exhibit. Encourage students to look at and study the dolls. Point out the simple three-dimensional forms that are observed in making the various dolls. Review and demonstrate how to construct a simple doll-like form. "How do the color, shape, and form create eye-catching miniature sculptures that reveal a specific culture?"

Process
1. Select a culture different from your own. Create a doll dressed in clothing (contemporary or historic) reflective of the culture. Shape a 1-oz. package of Model Magic into three-dimensional solids as the basic form from which to create the doll.
2. Model, pinch, and add texture to the basic form to extend design possibilities that might include arms, legs, heads, clothing, and additional cultural features. Air-dry 24 hours.
3. Dip watercolor pencils into water to soften. Color designs on the dried doll. Gently fill areas with watercolor washes and allow the decorated form to dry.
4. Gently apply a white glue glaze to dried doll. Air-dry the glaze.

Assessment
Ask students to identify three-dimensional forms observed in their doll. Invite students to exchange and study each other's dolls. Identify and chart the total number of simple three-dimensional forms that were used by the class to create all the dolls in class. Verify the accuracy of the representation.

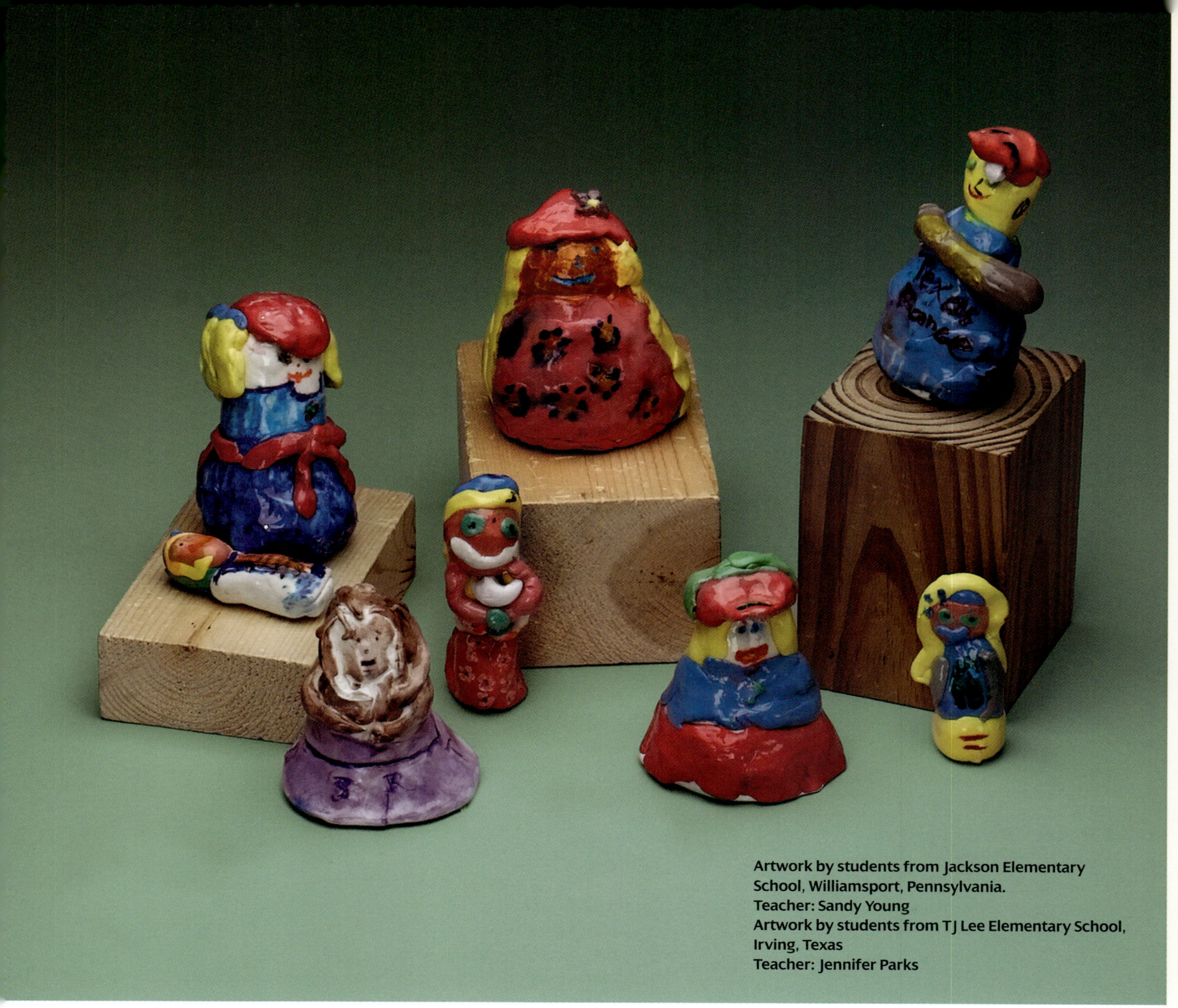

Artwork by students from Jackson Elementary School, Williamsport, Pennsylvania.
Teacher: Sandy Young
Artwork by students from TJ Lee Elementary School, Irving, Texas
Teacher: Jennifer Parks

Background Information

One of the most distinctively Russian crafts known today is the "Matryoshka," or nesting doll. Inside a large egg-shaped or cylindrical painted doll is another doll, and inside that is another. Although it is known worldwide as a "traditional" Russian craft, it is actually not much more than 100 years old.

The dolls were invented around 1890, in a workshop near Moscow. The artists and artisans, along with their patron, Sawa Mamontov, were dedicated to making works in an original Russian style, using traditional skills, designs and ideas, especially ones based on folk images and daily life. The idea is said to have been drawn from a combination of a doll brought back from Japan and the traditional Russian skill of turning wood to create nesting objects such as eggs.

What made each doll outstanding was the colorful painting that gave it features and clothing, often based on historical folk characters and costumes. The name "Matryoshka" was a popular woman's name at the time, at its root associated with the Latin word for mother ("mater"). The figure of the robust peasant woman sheltering her children is an endearing and eternal image of the loving and protective quality of motherhood.

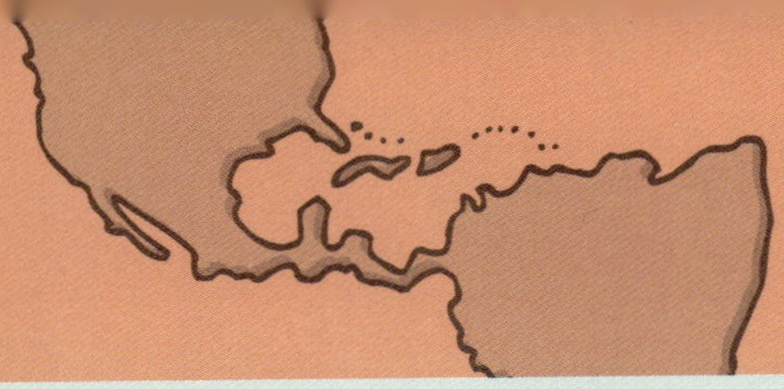

Map Your Space

Grade Level
K-2

Classroom Time
Two 40-min. periods

Materials/Tools
- Craft paper
- Crayola® Artista II® Tempera Paint
- Crayola Erasable Colored Pencils
- Crayola Gel FX Markers
- Crayola Paint Brushes
- Crayola Scissors
- Recycled newspaper
- Ribbon
- Ruler
- Water containers
- White tag board

Tips
Ask a parent volunteer to cut brown craft paper into 12" x 12" squares. Cover your painting area with newspaper. Avoid applying very thick amounts of paint to the paper surface when painting.

Resources
As the Crow Flies: A First Book of Maps by Gail Hartman
Mapping Penny's World by Loreen Leedy
Maps and Globes by Jack Knowlton
Me on the Map by Joan Sweeney

Visual Arts Standard 3
Choosing and evaluating a range and of subject matter, symbols, and ideas.

Social Studies Standard III
People, Places, and Environments

Objective
Students think about, identify, and map the contents of a room of their choice at school or at home.

Teacher Preparation
Classroom Teacher: Display maps of your school's neighborhood, city, and state in the classroom. Ask children to find where their school and homes are on the maps. Encourage them to bring in maps of places where they have been.

Art Teacher: Display historic and artistic map reproductions. Draw a simple map of the art room on a mural. Label major furnishings such as doors, windows, sinks, tables, and storage shelves.

Discussion Starters
Classroom Teacher: Read *Mapping Penny's World.* Discuss parts of maps. Explain concepts such as scale, estimation, direction, and symbols.

Art Teacher: Discuss the art room map. Point out the symbols and relationships among locations. Discuss how maps help you learn more about the area that is being mapped. Encourage students to notice texture, color, and relative size among objects on the map.

Process
1. Paint one side of the craft paper with decorative designs that include lines, dots, and textures. Air-dry the paint.
2. Choose a favorite room in your house, school, or other public place. Imagine you are a bird looking down at the room from the ceiling. What shape is the room? Where are the doors? Windows? Furniture?
3. Sketch a plan of your room and its furnishings from a bird's-eye view with Erasable Colored Pencils on white tag board. Erase to make corrections.
4. Use the colored pencil plan as your study to create a Gel-FX-marker map of your room on the side of the paper that does not have paint decorations.
5. Cut 12" of ribbon. Roll your paper into a cylinder with the map on the inside and the decorative paint design on the outside. Ask a friend to help you tie it into a scroll.

Assessment
Students exchange maps. Ask them to identify the mapped location and describe what is included in each room, based on the map's symbols. Consider the accuracy and clarity of maps.

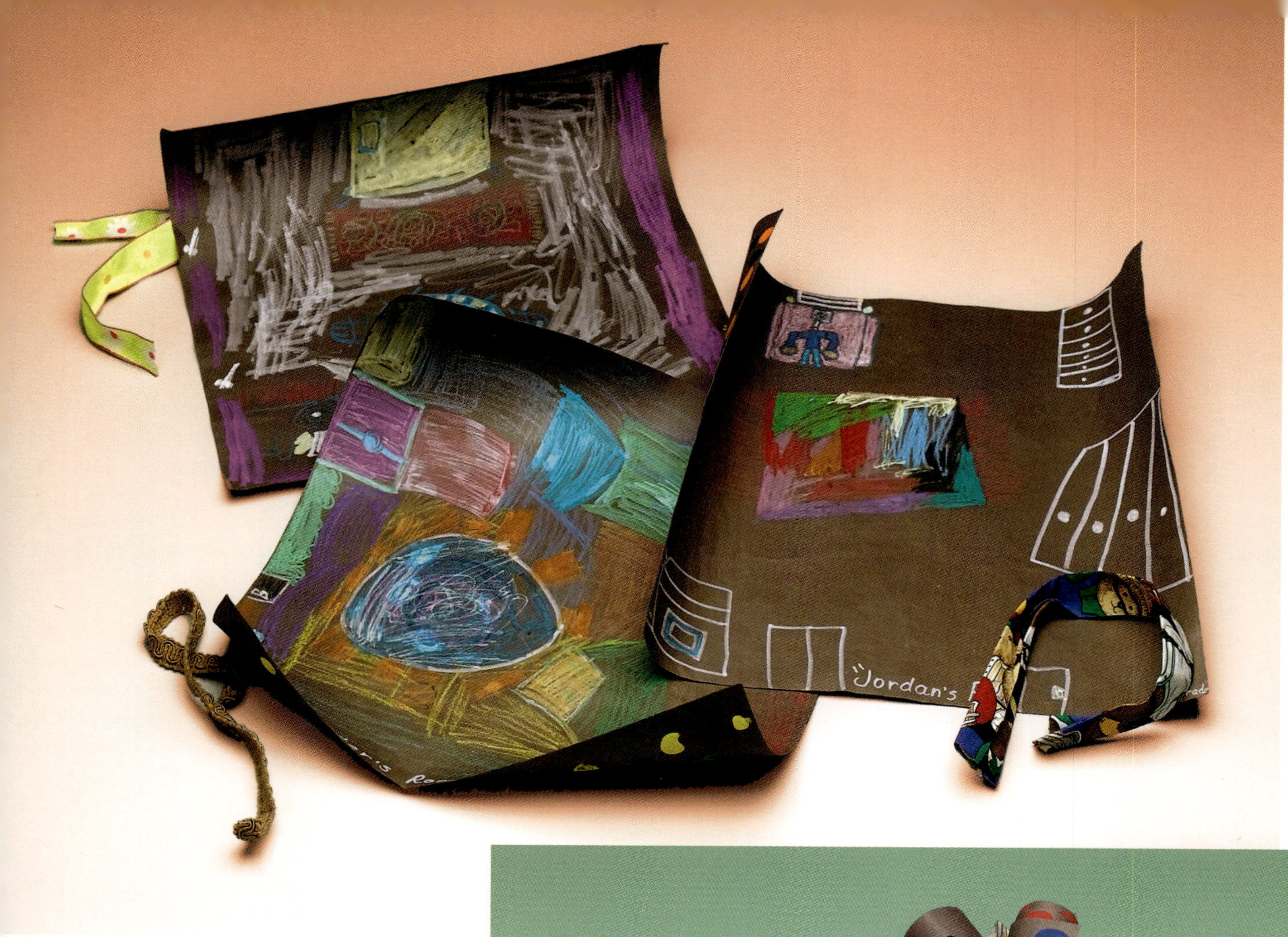

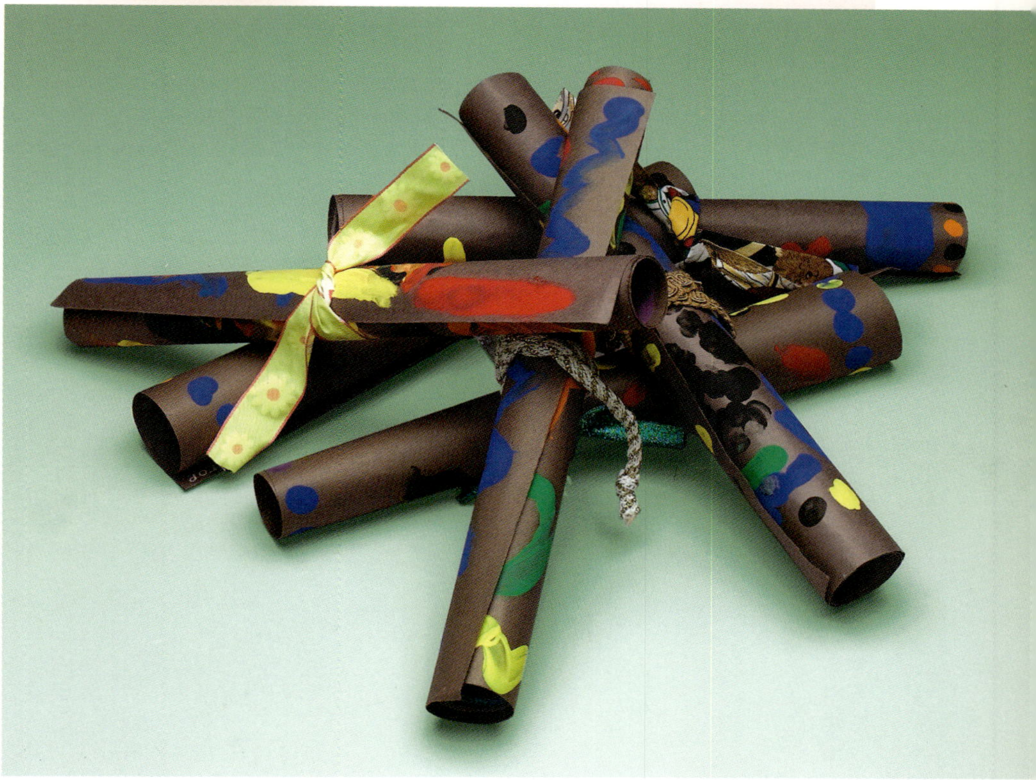

Artwork by students from Brenham Elementary School, Brenham, Texas.
Teacher: Marcia Elise Effinger

Background Information

Maps are an essential part of our lives. Can you imagine a time when there wasn't a map to help you get where you needed to go? The first known map was made in the Middle East, on a clay tablet small enough to fit in your hand. It was drawn between 2300 and 2500 BCE! That's more than 4000 years old. Experts think maps were probably drawn before then, although they haven't found any earlier examples.

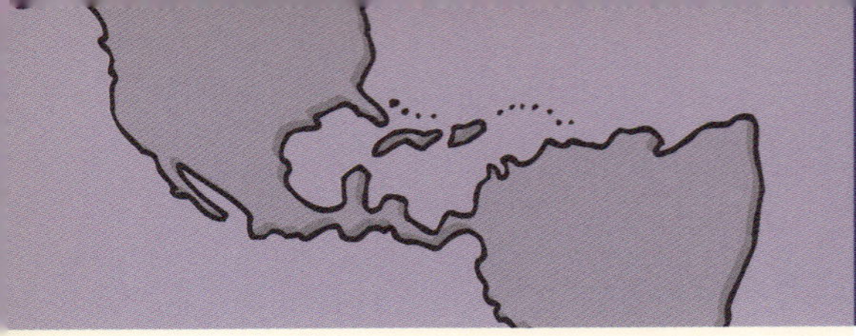

Business Card Business

Grade Level
3-4

Classroom Time
Two 40-min. periods

Materials/Tools
- Crayola® Erasable Colored Pencils
- Crayola Scissors
- Crayola Watercolor Brushes
- Crayola Watercolor Colored Pencils
- Recycled newspaper
- Water containers
- White drawing paper or tag board (12" x 18")
- White paper

Tips
Cover your painting area with newspaper. To maintain clean color, avoid over-brushing colors. Soften watercolor colored pencil tips by dipping or soaking them in water. Use hand-held sharpeners to refresh pencil tips.

Resources
A Basket of Bangles: How a Business Begins by Ginger Howard
General Store by Rachel Field
Market! by Ted Lewin
The Pot That Juan Built by Nancy Andrews-Goebel
Work by Ann Morris

Visual Arts Standard 5
Reflecting upon and assessing the characteristics and merits of their work and the work of others.

Social Studies Standard VII
Production, Distribution, and Consumption

Objective
Students create personalized business cards that link them to a profession or job involved in the production or exchange of goods and services.

Teacher Preparation
Classroom Teacher: Display books and tools relating to work, trade, and business. Encourage students to discuss the importance of selecting a business name, identifying jobs to be done, creating a budget, and making an organizational chart to support the business.

Art Teacher: Display reproductions of business cards, historic and current. Show cards that contain unique business names, attention-getting logos, employee names, and job titles that link directly to the business.

Discussion Starters
Classroom Teacher: Read *General Store* or a similar book. Choose teams with four or five students each. Teams should cooperate to identify an imaginary business that supports and promotes their school. Teams have to select a business name and identify jobs and titles. Each team collaborates to make three thumbnail sketches for business cards using erasable colored pencils. Include the following:

- The business name
- The student's name and job title
- An eye-catching graphic or logo for the business

Art Teacher: Show the business card display. Look at and discuss cards that immediately capture attention. Talk about how teams might redesign a card so that it communicates their business more effectively. Encourage teams to rethink and revise their individual sketches.

Process
1. Choose the most promising thumbnail sketch that your team created and refine it. Use erasable colored pencils so you can easily make revisions.
2. Enlarge the design on drawing paper using watercolor pencils. Include the business name, slogan, logo, employee name, and job title.
3. Enrich the design by using a damp brush to fill shapes with watercolor.

Assessment
Encourage students to analyze and then rank all the business cards for their visual impact and communication strengths. Summarize learning.

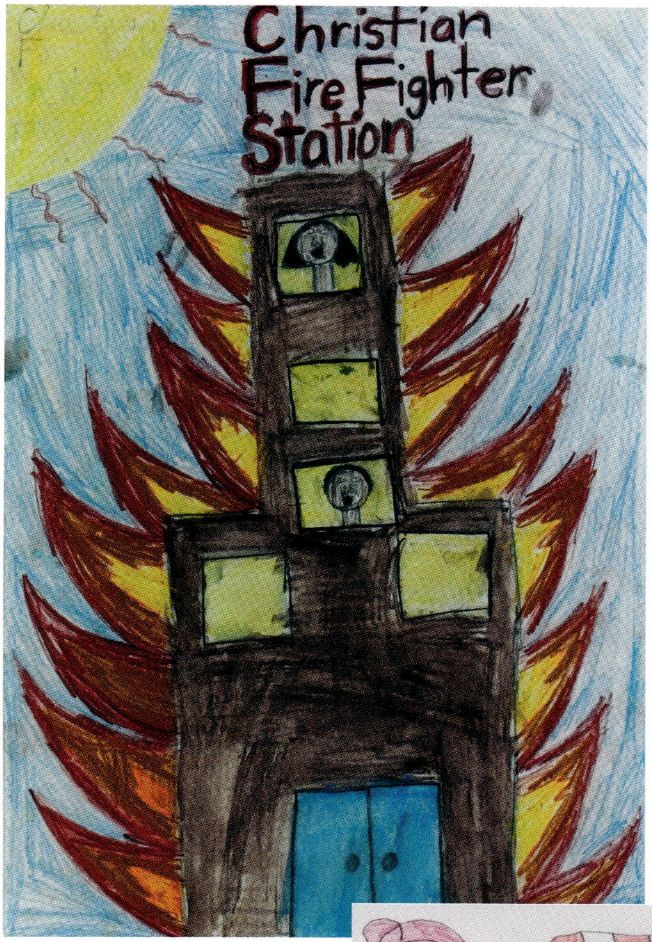

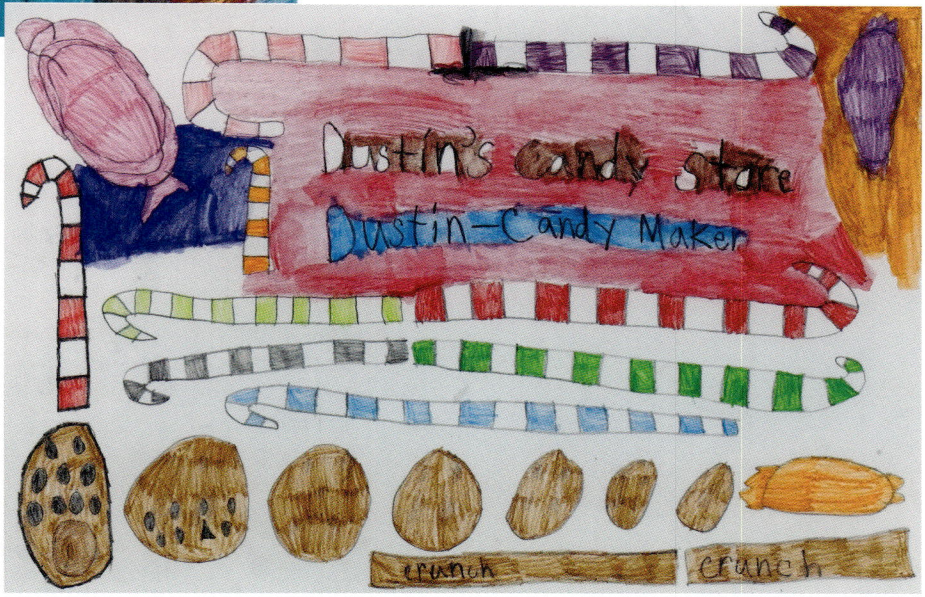

Artwork by students from Sandy Plains Elementary School, Baltimore, Maryland.
Teacher: Jen O'Flaherty

Background Information

Graphic design and advertising are essential for any business's visibility. With designs and symbols, businesses have been able to promote their products to all parts of the world. However, global advertising has to be approached cautiously, because translation and cultural differences can skew the meaning of an ad. For instance, a red symbol in the United States might represent something dangerous or hot. In China, red means happiness or marriage! In Uzbekistan, a popular laundry detergent is called Barf. Why? Because in the Tajik language, barf means snow. Many symbols have become familiar throughout the world. You can see McDonald's golden arches in more than 120 countries.

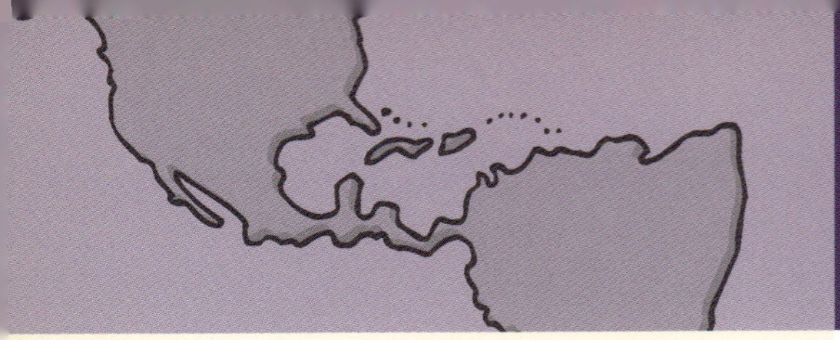

Campaign for Office of "Leader"

Grade Level
3-4

Classroom Time
Two 40-min. periods

MATERIALS/TOOLS
- Crayola® Classic Markers
- Crayola Erasable Colored Pencils
- Crayola Fine Line Markers
- Crayola Scissors
- Masking tape
- Oak tag
- White paper

Tip
Use tag board, cardboard, or posterboard to create campaign buttons and badges.

Resources
A Very Important Day by Maggie Rugg Herold
Rescuing a Neighborhood: The Bedford-Stuyvesant
So You Want to be President? by Weston Woods
Volunteer Ambulance Corps by Robert Fleming

Visual Arts Standard 5
Reflecting upon and assessing the characteristics and merits of their work and the work of others.

Social Studies Standard VI
Power, Authority, and Governance

Objective
Students create campaign posters, banners, signs, and buttons to help convince their classmates to support their candidacy for "Community Leader."

Teacher Preparation
Classroom Teacher: Display political campaign photographs. Invite students to talk about elections with which they are familiar. Discuss the U.S. election process. Explain how candidates campaign to convince voters that they are qualified for a public service job.

Art Teacher: Display political campaign posters, pamphlets, buttons, and other campaign artifacts. Invite students to talk about why the artifacts catch attention and help people make personal voting decisions. Discuss the importance of color, attention-getting slogans, and other visual effects in helping to capture votes.

Discussion Starters
Classroom Teacher: "In our society, being a leader is important. Thomas Jefferson believed that Americans should campaign for the 'Office of Citizen' to support the government. It is ou responsibility to support the common good. All of us are responsible for respecting diversity, volunteering, joining community organizations, voting, and serving on juries. Think about campaigning for the office of 'Community Leader.' What would you need to do in order to be elected?"

Art Teacher: "Study the campaign objects in our class display. What parts of these objects catch our attention? What colors, shapes, lines, and textures do we pay attention to? How would you change or redesign the objects that we pay the least amount of attention to? Create an election campaign that includes posters and badges to help you capture votes for the 'Community Leader' in your class."

Process
Create a campaign poster

1. Sketch poster ideas with erasable colored pencils on paper. You can easily erase to make changes.
2. Include images that symbolize the qualities that you will bring to office if elected.
3. Finalize your ideas. Scale up the drawing on oak tag using fine line markers.
4. Draw attention to the poster by filling shapes and spaces with marker color.

Design a campaign button

1. Cut circles from oak tag. Lightly write a campaign slogan on the circle with erasable colored pencils. Erase and make corrections as necessary.
2. Trace over your final slogan with fine line markers. Fill shapes with marker color.
3. Stick campaign buttons to clothing with masking tape loops.

Assessment
Conduct a classroom election for "Community Leader." Measure the effectiveness of campaig materials by asking students to cast ballots based on candidates' campaigns' visual appeal. Summarize learning.

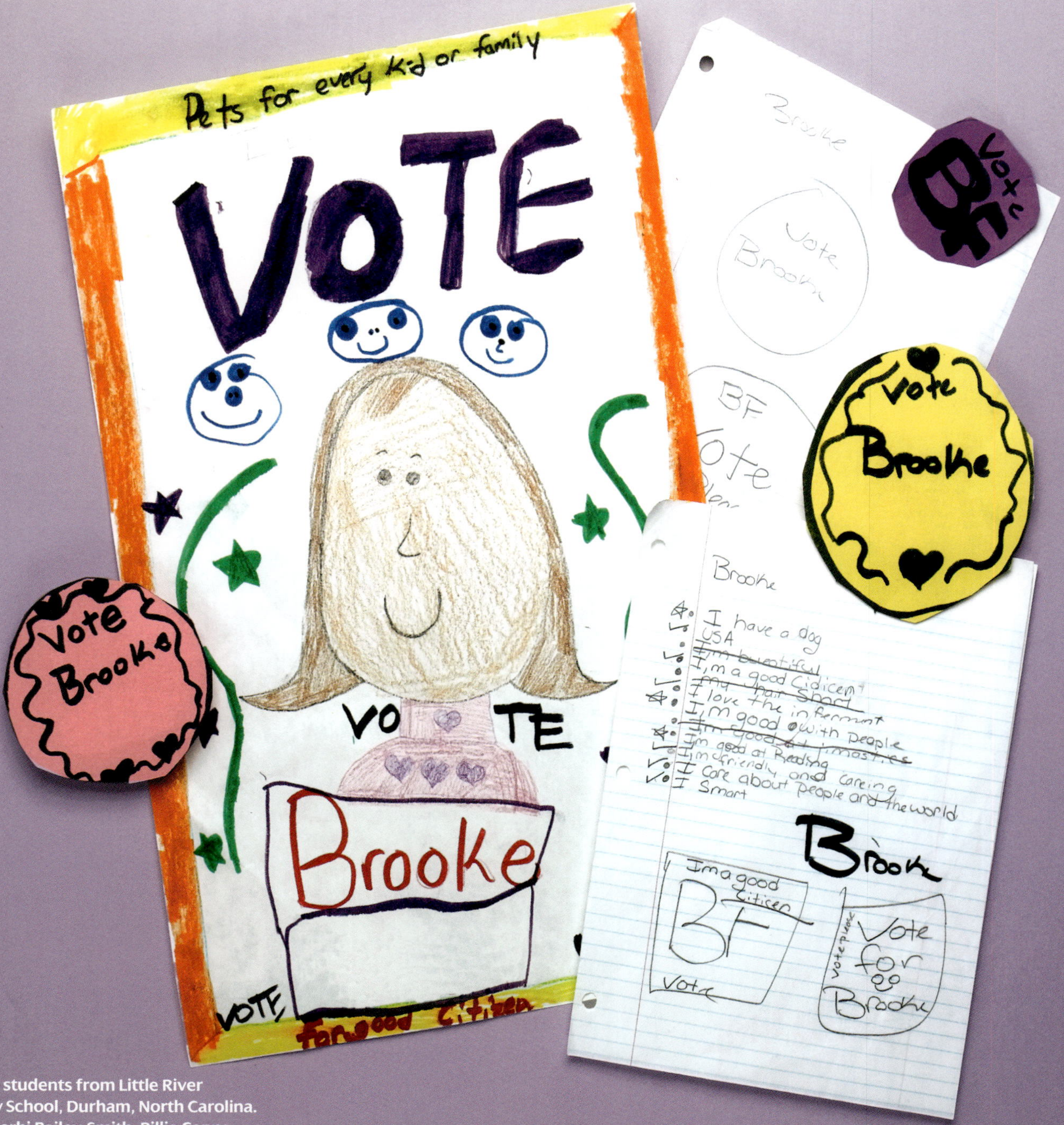

Artwork by students from Little River Elementary School, Durham, North Carolina. Teachers: Barbi Bailey-Smith; Billie Capps

Background Information

Cornell University Libraries house the Susan H. Douglas Collection of Political Americana in their Division of Rare and Manuscript Collections. The collection consists of approximately 5,500 pieces of political memorabilia dating from 1789 to 1960 in the following categories: ballots, bric-a-brac (larger three-dimensional objects), broadsides, buttons, cartoons, maps and charts, pamphlets, paper miscellaneous, parade items, posters, prints, ribbons, sheet music, songbooks, textiles, trinkets, and wearing apparel. All the contents were used for presidential elections, and one can witness the culture and people of the time reflected through the design of the artifacts.

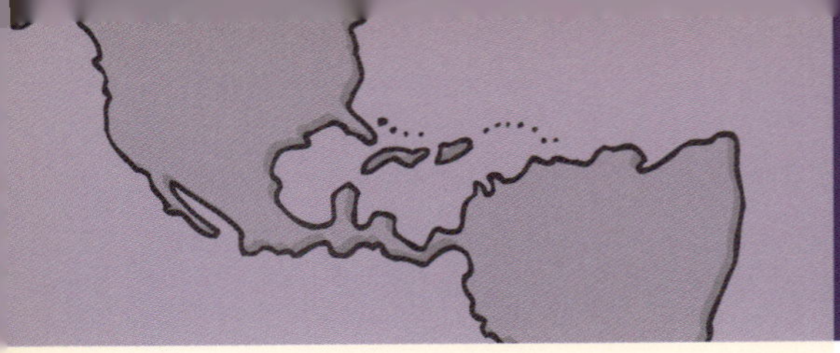

Let's Go Letterbox Hunting

Grade Level
3-4

Classroom Time
Three or four 40-min. periods

Materials/Tools
- Clean household sponges
- Clean plastic spray bottle
- Craft paper
- Crayola® Glitter Glue
- Crayola Model Magic® (white)
- Crayola School Glue
- Crayola So Big® Paint Brushes
- Crayola Tempera Paint
- Crayola Twistables® Crayons
- Oak tag (9" x 12")
- Plastic dinnerware
- Recycled cardboard boxes with lids (small)
- Recycled clean combs
- Recycled newspaper
- Ribbon or yarn
- Water containers
- White paper

Tips
Ask for volunteers to collect recycled boxes. Invite parent or student volunteers to mix glue and water solution in clean, plastic pump spray containers. Cover painting areas with newspaper.

Resources
Hidden Treasures: Amazing Stories of Discovery by Tina Holdcroft
The Letters Are Lost by Lisa Campbell Ernst
The Letter Jesters by Cathryn Falwell

Visual Arts Standard 2
Using knowledge of structures and functions.

Social Studies Standard III
People, Places, and Environment

Objective
Students design a passport book and maps with clues that lead the way to a hidden letterbox.

Teacher Preparation
Classroom Teacher: Display assorted maps, atlases, and books about scavenger or treasure hunts.

Art Teacher: Create a sample letterbox, stamp, passport book, and a map to help students understand the activity.

Discussion Starters
Classroom Teacher: Challenge students to hypothesize reasons for maps. How are maps used other than to provide travel directions? How could maps contain clues that can lead people to treasures?

Art Teacher: Explain the letterbox practice of collecting stamps in a passport book (see Background Information). Help students understand that clues on maps can lead collectors on adventures.

Process
Design Monoprints
1. Spread a thin layer of tempera paint evenly over oak tag paper.
2. Blend colors gently using brushes, then etch into paint using plastic combs or forks to make textures. Explore design possibilities.
3. Press a second sheet of paper over the etched paint design immediately to create a monoprint, and set it aside to dry.
4. Create a water and glue solution that is easily sprayed through a spray bottle nozzle. Experiment with water-to-glue proportions, as spray nozzle sizes may vary.
5. Coat the dried monoprint with a mist of glue solution and set aside to dry.
6. Repeat the process to create additional prints for passport covers and to cover letterboxes. Rinse spray bottle clean after use.

Decorate a Letterbox
1. Cut or tear shapes of monoprint paper and then glue them to the outside of a lidded box.

Make Passports
1. Fold a dried monoprint in half to create a passport book cover. Fold three or four sheets of paper in half and insert inside the cover fold.
2. Tie ribbon or yarn around the folds to hold the pages inside the cover.

Create a Stamp and Stamp Pad
1. Form Model Magic to make a thick replica of your first initial. Gently tap the letter against a flat surface to make a smooth stamping surface. Air dry the stamp.
2. Apply and then brush out small amounts of tempera paint over a clean, moist kitchen sponge to create a paint-filled pad to use when you are ready to stamp passports.
3. Press the dried letter stamps on the paint-covered pad to coat the letter with color.
4. Press the paint coated letter stamps on the pages in the passports when the boxes are found.

Draw a Map
1. Decide where to hide your letterbox. Use Twistables to draw a map containing visual symbols that can lead others to your hidden letterbox.
2. Write text clues that support the visual clues on back of the map.

Assessment
Hide letterboxes, each containing a letter stamp and a marker. Challenge students to search for letterboxes and offer proof of their discovery by stamping their passport books with stamps they find. Continue until all letterboxes are discovered. Summarize learning.

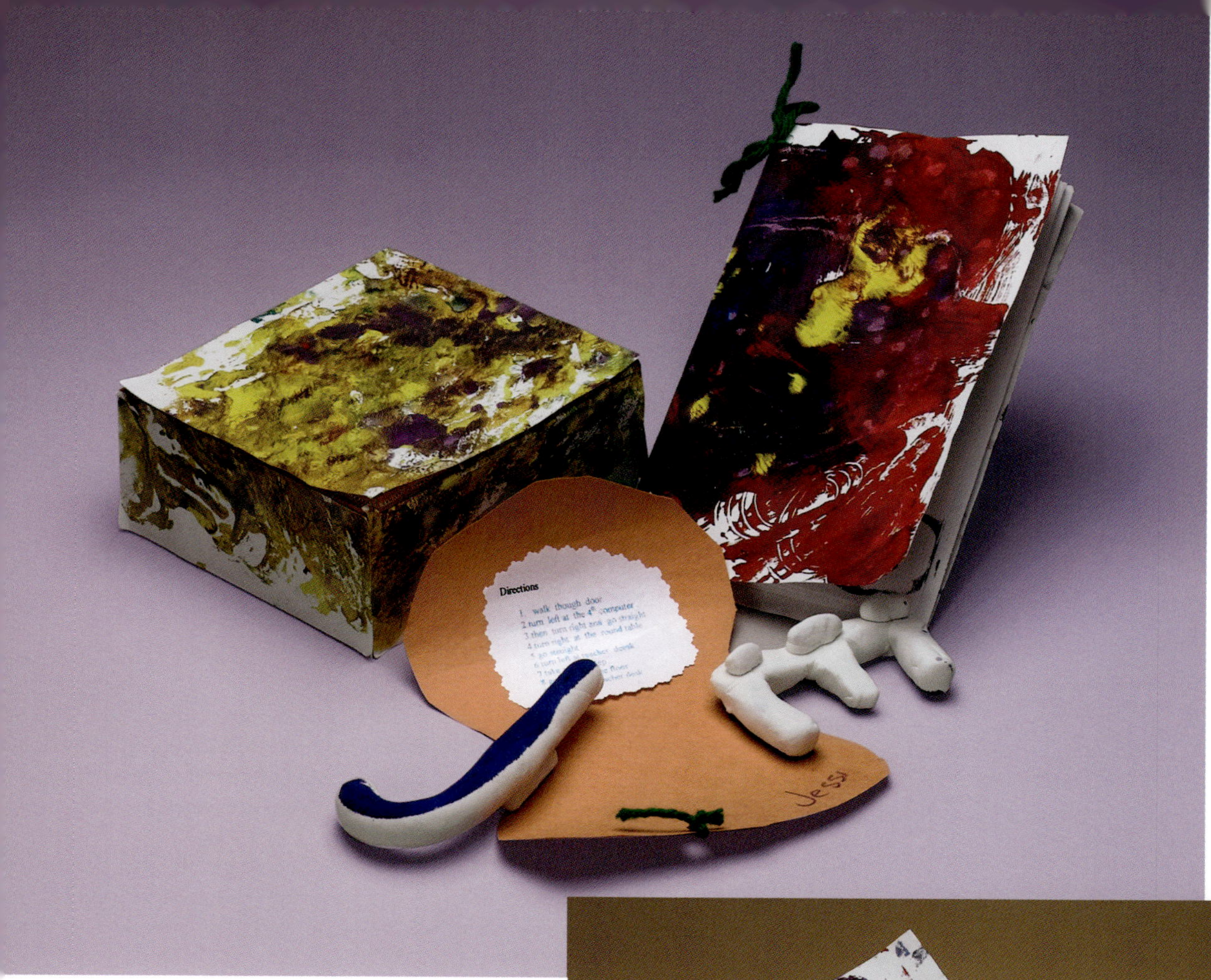

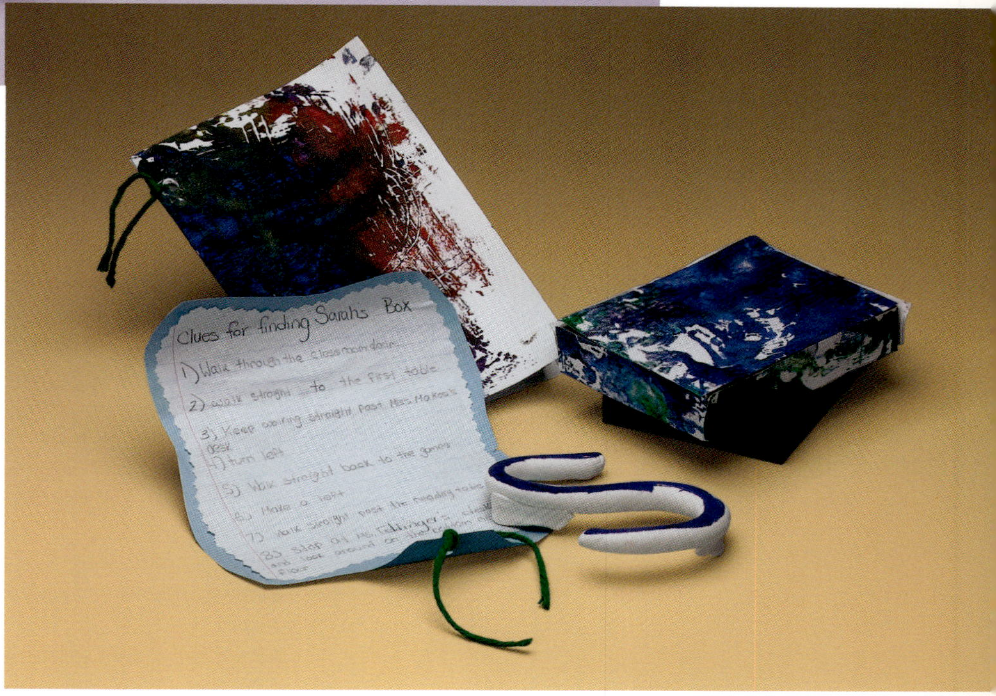

Artwork by students from Saucon Valley Middle School, Hellertown, Pennsylvania.
Teacher: Jenna Makos

Background Information

Letterboxing originated in England and is a hobby that is catching on in the United States. Letterboxing combines orienteering, rubber stamp collecting, and creativity for a unique hobby that everyone can enjoy. The object is to collect stamps that are hidden in various locations. The locations of letterboxes are found on letterboxing Websites and include detailed, but tricky clues and maps. Finding the boxes is a challenge and makes collecting them even more exciting. Gatherings of letterbox stamps collectors occur at cafes where the collectors share their adventures and stamps. This fascinating hobby is like a modern-day treasure hunt!

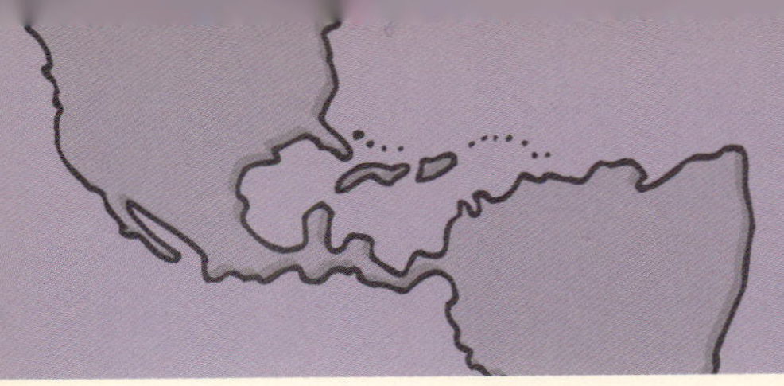

We Are the Children

Grade Level
3-4

Classroom Time
Two or three 40-min. periods

Materials/Tools
- Collage materials
- Construction paper (12" x 18")
- Craft paper (3' x 6')
- Crayola® Artista II® Tempera
- Crayola Colored Pencil Classpack®
- Crayola Construction Paper™ Crayons
- Crayola Gel FX Markers
- Crayola Glue Sticks
- Crayola Paint Brushes
- Crayola Scissors
- Fabric scraps
- Recycled magazines
- Recycled newspaper

Tip
Ask student volunteers to help paint the large world map mural. Cover the art area with newspaper.

Resources
All the Colors of the Earth by Sheila Hamanaka
Black Is Brown Is Tan by Arnold Adoff
Coming to America: A Muslim Family's Story by Bernard Wolf
Hands on Arts and Crafts: Collage by Anthony Hodge
Immigrants by Yale Strom
Quilted Landscape: Conversations With Young
The Colors of Us by Karen Katz

Visual Arts Standard 4
Understanding the visual arts in relation to arts and cultures.

Social Studies Standard IX
Global Connections

Objective
Students create decorative paper-doll children that reflect their knowledge and understanding of Romare Bearden's collage art and the features observed in historical and contemporary dress in other cultures.

Teacher Preparation
Classroom Teacher: Collect photographs and books that show and describe traditional and contemporary authentic dress (both everyday and special occasion) from various cultures.

Art Teacher: Display paper dolls, clothing designs from other cultures and time periods, and reproductions of Romare Bearden's collage art. Paint on craft paper (or obtain) a large world map to display children's paper dolls.

Discussion Starters
Classroom Teacher: Read portions of *Quilted Landscape: Conversations With Young Immigrants* or similar material. Discuss how people throughout the world dress differently and why. Make a list to identify similarities and differences in dress among at least three cultures including those of families in your community. Research design styles to check for accuracy.

Art Teacher: Show *Hands on Arts and Crafts: Collage.* "Romare Bearden used collage art to create images representative of his culture. Study Bearden's collages. What do you notice about them? How does he create people and scenes? Collage art combines materials to create new images. The materials are cut, arranged, and glued together to create new designs."

Process
Create paper dolls

1. Fold colored construction paper in half, joining the short ends. Fold the top edge back to the crease. Turn the paper over and fold on the opposite side to create an accordion fold. Place the paper in a vertical position.
2. Draw a simple figure on the top accordion fold, making sure that hands and feet extend to the edges of both sides of the paper.
3. Cut along the lines. Open to reveal paper dolls. Cut apart and glue dolls together to create groups of dolls that vary in number.

Decorate the dolls

1. Cut and glue facial features from recycled magazines onto dolls heads so the designs reflect and illustrate a similarity to the collage technique of Romare Bearden.
2. Color, cut out, and glue on decorated paper or fabric clothes that reflect various cultures.
3. Enrich clothing designs by adding Gel FX marker, Construction Paper Crayon, and glitter glue designs to paper surface.

Display the dolls

1. Attach paper dolls to the world map so they all join hands.

Assessment
Challenge students to identify the cultural heritage of their dolls based on the design of the clothing. Verify the accuracy of the clothing. Summarize learning.

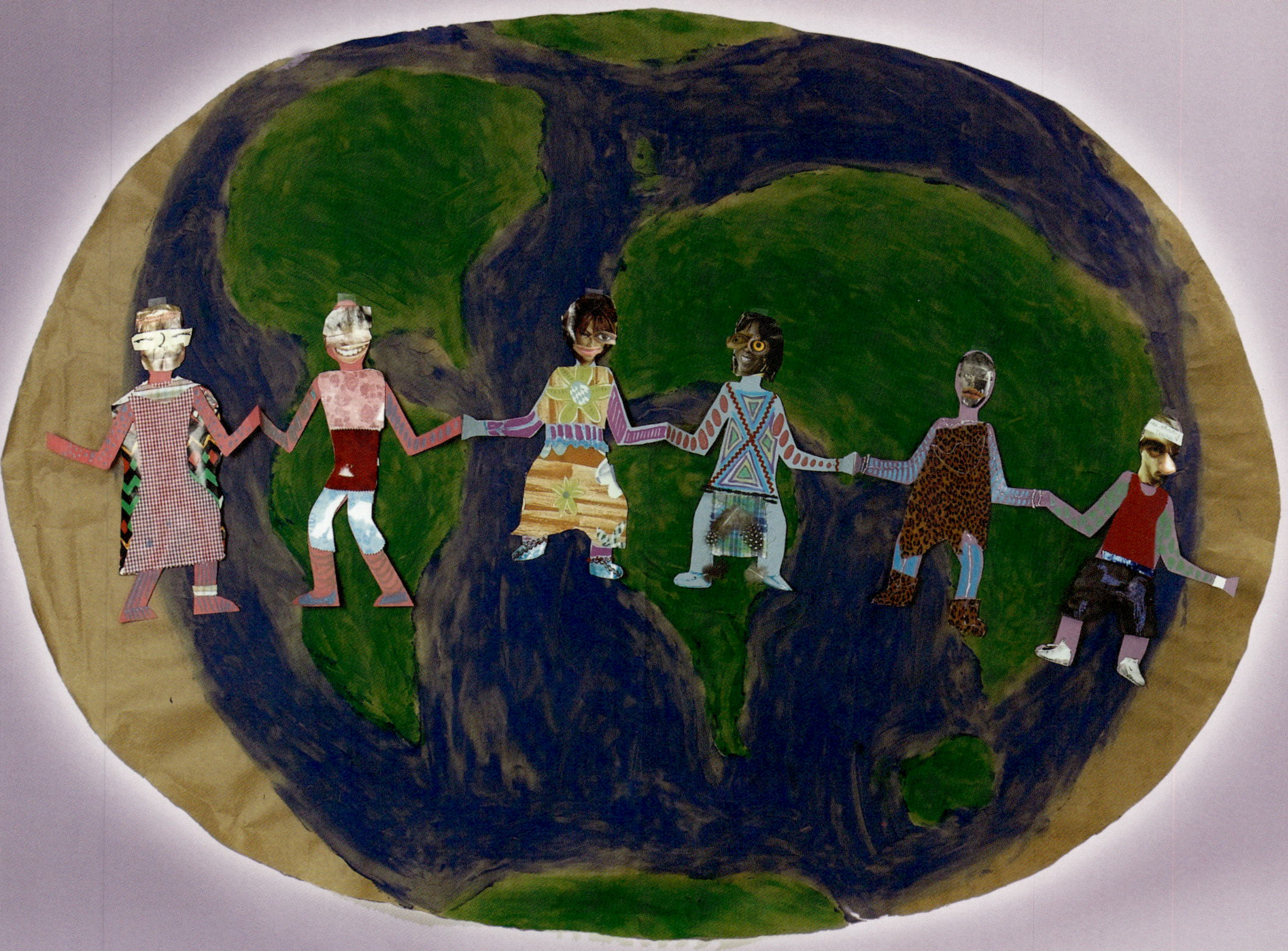

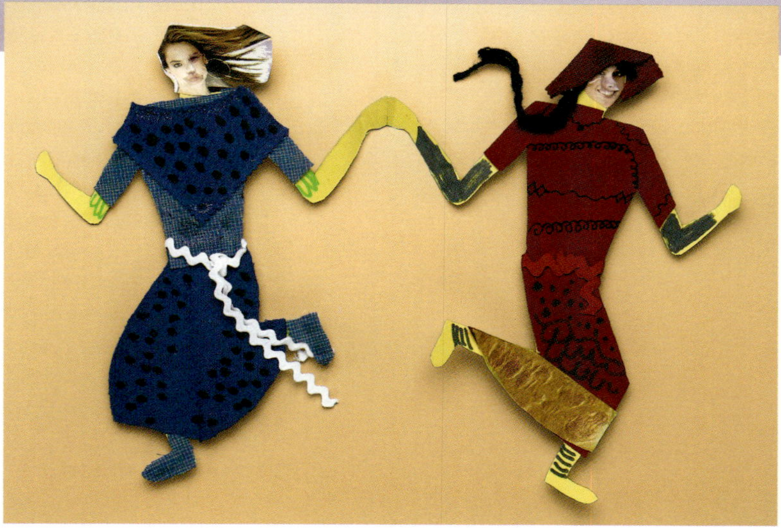

Artwork by students from CS 102,
Bronx, New York.
Teacher: Neila Steiner

Background Information

Romare Bearden used collage to create images that reflected the lifestyles and social rituals of his African American heritage. Art was his instrument to create social change. He embedded his collages with symbols that added meaning to his work and the story being told through it. Art was his instrument to create social change. Jazz and the blues were major influences, and he compared the improvisational quality of jazz to his arrangement and use of color in his collages.

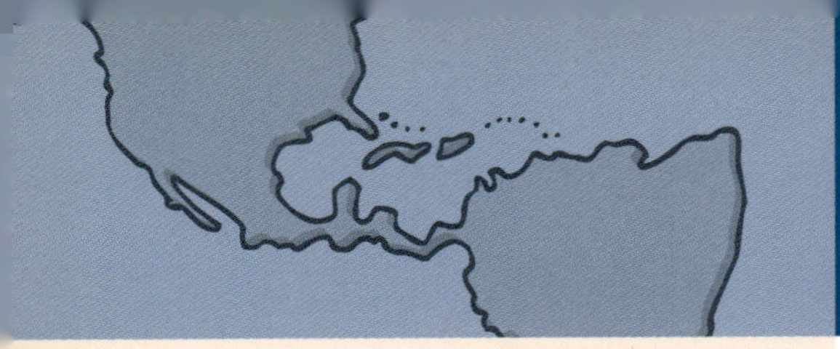

Action Makes Dreams Come True

Grade Level
5-6

Classroom Time
Three to four 40-min. periods

Materials/Tools
- Construction paper
- Crayola® Erasable Colored Pencils
- Crayola Oil Pastels
- Crayola School Glue
- Crayola Scissors
- Drawing paper
- Recycled boxes with lids
- Recycled paint brushes
- Ribbon or yarn
- White paper

Tip
Ask parent volunteers to collect recycled ribbon and boxes with lids.

Resources
Going Green: A Kid's Handbook to Saving the Planet by John Elkington
Harvesting Hope: The Story of Cesar Chavez by Kathleen Krull
Martin's Big Words: The Life of Dr. Martin Luther King, Jr. by Doreen Rappaport
The New Nation by Joy Hakim
The Picture Book of Thomas Jefferson by David A. Alder

Visual Arts Standard 6
Making connections between visual arts and other disciplines.

Social Studies Standard X
Civic Ideals and Practices

Objective
Students create "Action Makes Dreams Come True" containers that identify a social issue. They collect suggested solutions from classmates in the boxes.

Teacher Preparation
Classroom Teacher: Display books and posters about individuals who identified and worked to correct social concerns. Two examples are Cesar Chavez, who helped U.S. migrant farmworkers get better working conditions, and the Rev. Dr. Martin Luther King, Jr., who worked for civil rights for African Americans.

Art Teacher: Collect boxes with visual imagery on the outside as examples of box decoration. Create an "Action Makes Dreams Come True" box that illustrates a social issue that needs to be addressed. Ask friends to contribute solutions to include in your box.

Discussion Starters
Classroom Teacher: Read *My Brother Martin* or a similar book about an advocate for change. Introduce other individuals who changed the country the or world for the better. Discuss social change and how people's dreams helped shape the way we live today. "Do you know anyone who dreams of helping the world? What can you do to improve your community, your country, or the world?"

Art Teacher: Show students examples of decorated boxes. What symbols or images best draw attention to a social concern? Decorate your box so it captures the attention of classmates and encourages them to offer solutions to help address your cause.

Process
Create "Actions Make Dreams Come True" Boxes
1. Place the lid of a box on white drawing paper. Trace around the lid with an erasable colored pencil. (You may want to decorate the box's sides, too.)
2. Cut around the outlined shape. On it, use erasable colored pencils to sketch ideas that illustrate a social problem. Erase to make corrections where necessary.
3. Fill in the colored pencil drawing with oil pastel color.
4. Glue the finished design to the box lid. Place the box lid on the box.

Design Solution Scrolls
1. Review all the "Actions Make Dreams Come True" boxes. Select at least three that address social problems you wish to help solve.
2. Write each solution on paper. Roll each paper into a cylinder. Tie with ribbon or yarn. Place your solution inside the appropriate boxes.
3. Display the solutions from your box. Find ways to take action whenever possible by working with your community.

Assessment
Ask students to check the scrolls to make sure that the solutions help solve the problem illustrated on the lid. Did the illustrations generate creative, realistic solutions? Summarize learning.

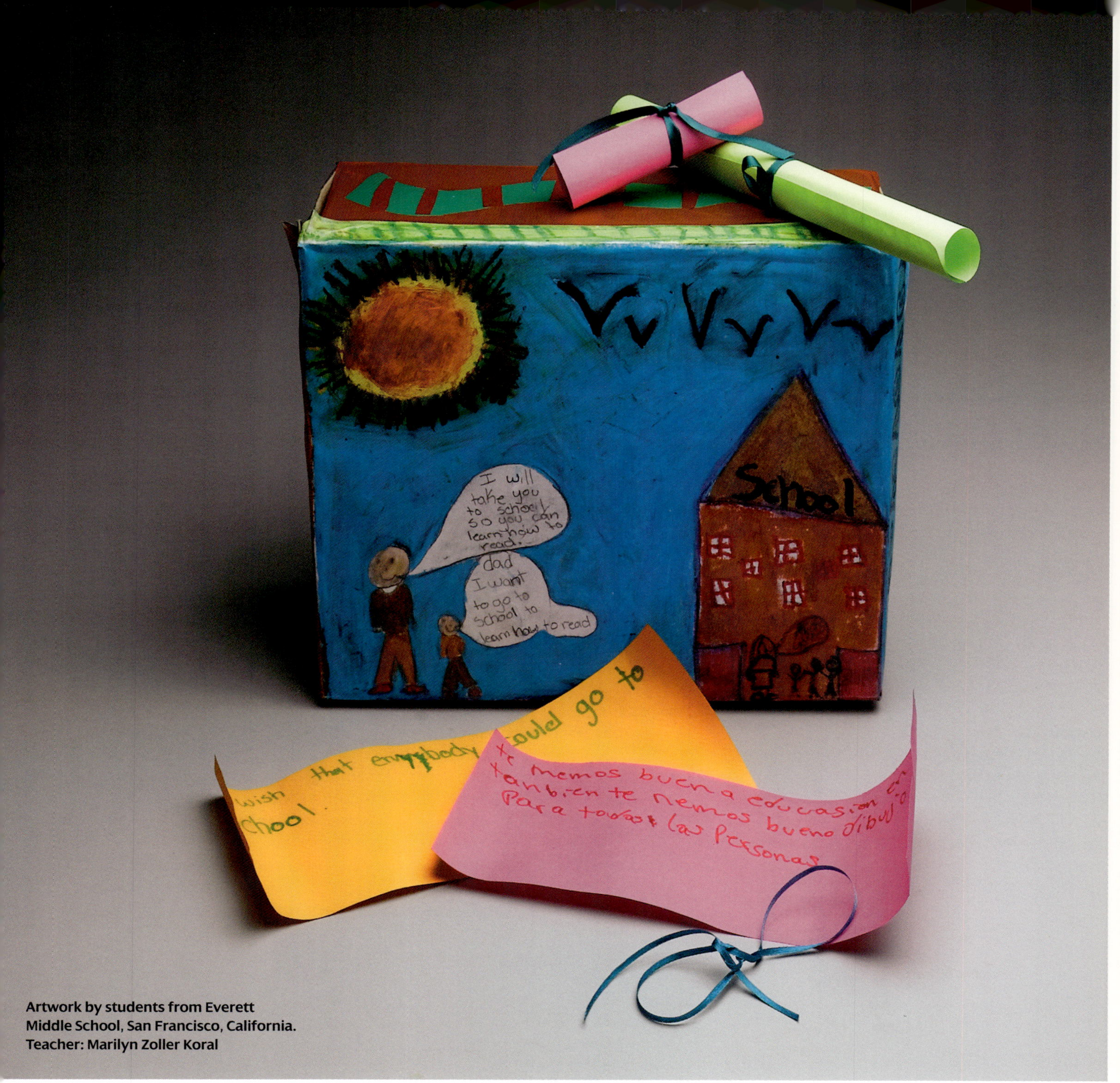

Artwork by students from Everett Middle School, San Francisco, California.
Teacher: Marilyn Zoller Koral

Background Information

Many cultures believe that putting dreams in boxes will help the dreamers capture their dreams. A Native American legend about a Dream Box states that if you put your dream in a box, hold it before you go to bed, and wish with all your heart for it to come true, when you get up in the morning, your dream will come true.

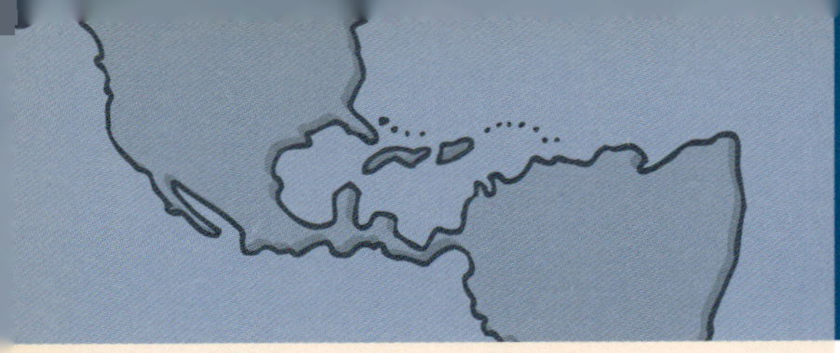

Noticeable Norens–Make Certain It Is on the Curtain

Grade Level
5-6

Classroom Time
Two 40-min. periods

Materials/Tools
- Crayola® Erasable Colored Pencils
- Crayola Fabric Markers
- Crayola School Glue
- Crayola Scissors
- Rulers
- White cotton panels
- White paper (letter and legal size)
- Yarn or ribbon

Tip
Ask parent or student volunteers to recycle and cut clean, plain recycled cotton or 50/50 cotton/polyester sheets into 18" by 24" panels (one for each team). Sheets or similar fabric also can be purchased at discount stores.

Resources
Japan for Kids: The Ultimate Guide for Parents and Their Children by Diane Wiltshire
Pictorial Encyclopedia of Japanese Life and Events edited by Anzai Tatsuo
The Way We Do It in Japan by Geneva Cobb Iijima

Visual Arts Standard 6
Making connections between visual arts and other disciplines.

Social Studies Standard IX
Global Connections

Objective
Students create team norens (Japanese-style curtains) containing symbols and signs that advertise a local, regional, national, or international business and the products or inventions that the business markets.

Teacher Preparation
Classroom Teacher: Set up a display with a title such as "Businesses and the Products They Market." Create sections for local, regional, national, and international entries.

Art Teacher: Ask students to help create a display of business logos from recycled magazines. Include among the logos Japanese family crests, signs, and symbols that typically are found on Japanese norens.

Discussion Starters
Classroom Teacher: Discuss the definitions of local, regional, national, and international. Invite students to identify and bring samples of products or ads for businesses to display in the appropriate categories.

Art Teacher: Ask students to define advertising. Invite them to share what they know about logos, signs, and symbols. Explain that Japanese stores use norens to advertise their products or services. Talk about the design qualities that make a good logo.

Process
1. Divide into groups of 3 or 4 to invent a business and a product to market. Cooperatively decide on a business name.
2. Design a noren that contains the following: business name, logo, signs or symbols, and a visual that identifies what product(s) the business will market.
3. Sketch ideas for your team noren with erasable colored pencils. Modify designs by erasing. Decide on the best design.
4. Draw the final advertisement on a cloth panel using fabric markers.
5. Roll legal-size paper into a tight cylinder (begin to roll at a corner to make the cylinder about 18" long). Glue closed. Cut 24" of yarn or ribbon and thread it through the cylinder.
6. Glue the noren to the cylinder. Air-dry and display the norens.

Assessment
Interview students and teachers from other classes to see if they can identify the products from the noren advertising. Check to see that all norens include a business name, logo, and sign or symbol that relate to the name and the product advertised. Summarize learning.

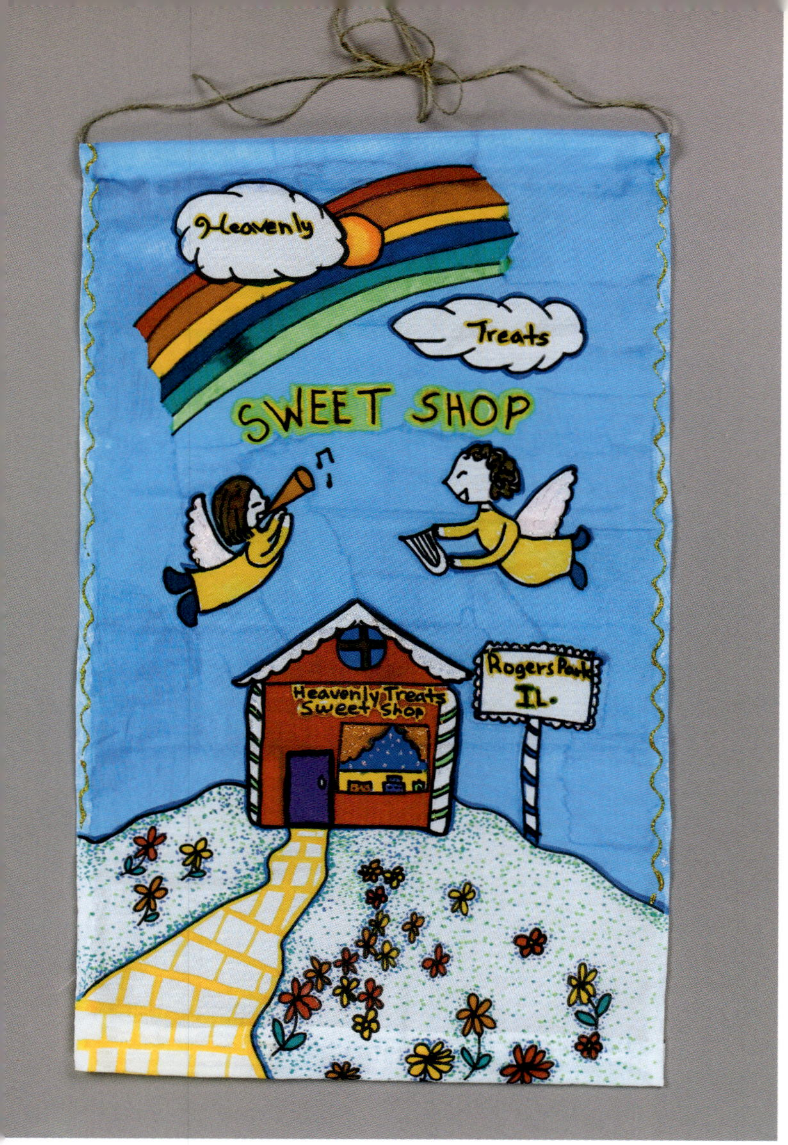

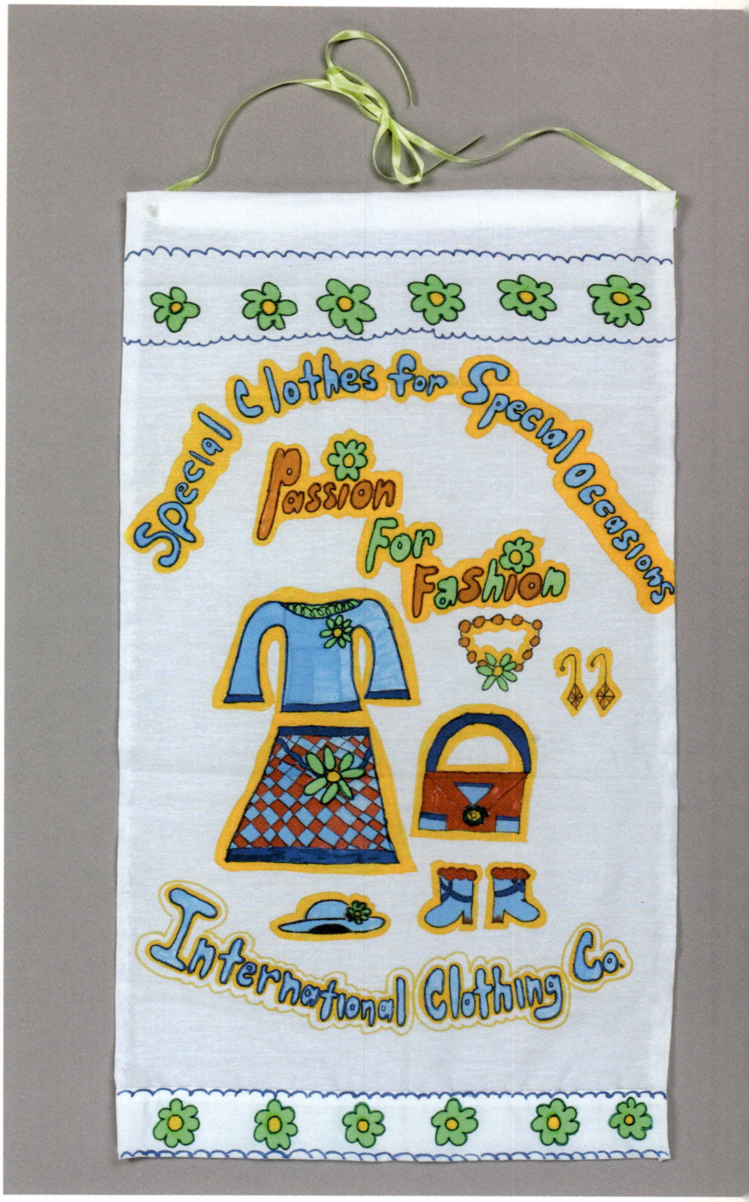

Artwork by students from Jordan Community School, Chicago, Illinois. Teacher: Elyse Martin

Background Information

The English translation of *noren* is "shop curtain". In Japan, norens hang in storefronts, advertising what products or services are inside. The art of making these shop curtains originally involved a tie-dying process done by hand. Shopkeepers carefully pick designs for their norens, because this is the first thing that greets visitors to their businesses. Just as norens are a popular art form in Japan, the idea of advertising remains an art form all over the world. Savvy graphic designers, advertisers, and business owners create universally recognized symbols and designs to attract customers.

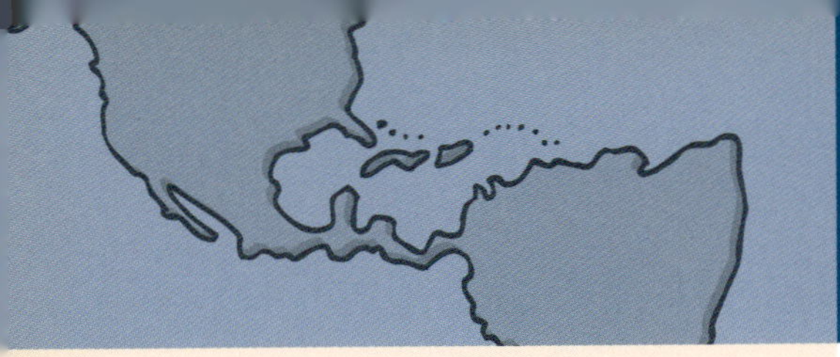

Rosa Takes a Freedom Ride

Grade Level
5-6

Classroom Time
Three 40-min. periods

Materials/Tools
- Crayola® Marker Classpack®
- Crayola Model Magic® Classpack (white)
- Crayola School Glue
- Crayola Scissors
- Crayola Watercolor Colored Pencil
- Classpack
- Crayola Watercolor Brushes
- Crayola Watercolors
- Recycled cardboard boxes
- Recycled magazines
- Recycled newspaper
- White paper

Tips
Ask the school staff and families to save and cut out 18" x 24" or larger flat corrugated cardboard sheets. Collect one per child. Cover the painting surface with newspaper.

Resources
Dear Mrs. Parks: A Dialogue With Today's Youth by Rosa Parks with Gregory J. Reed
If a Bus Could Talk: The Story of Rosa Parks by Faith Ringgold
Oh Freedom! Kids Talk About the Civil Rights Movement With the People Who Made It Happen by Casey King and Linda Barnett Osbourne
Rosa Parks: My Story by Rosa Parks
The Year They Walked: Rosa Parks and the Montgomery Bus Boycott by Beatrice Siegel

Visual Arts Standard 3
Choosing and evaluating a range of subject matter, symbols, and ideas.

Social Studies Standard II
Time, Continuity, and Change

Objective
Students study and then create a three-dimensional, installation-like, interactive time line that illustrates events associated with the United States civil rights movement.

Teacher Preparation
Classroom Teacher: Create a display about "Rosa Takes a Freedom Ride." Ask students to help collect, mount, and post pictures of Rosa Parks and other prominent African American figures of the time. Ask students to organize a timeline to illustrate the sequence of events associated with the civil rights movement, including what led up to Rosa Parks' ride and what happened after it.

Art Teacher: Create a bulletin board with a title such as "Riding Along With African American Artists." Include reproductions of Romare Bearden's collage art and other African American artists' images. Photocopy black and white images from magazines of people, places, and things for collages.

Discussion Starters
Classroom Teacher: Ask students to think about the history of African Americans in the United States. Challenge students to research events that led up to Rosa Parks' decision to sit in the "whites only" section of a city bus. Then ask students to report back findings.

Art Teacher: Ask students to describe what they see when they look at Romare Bearden's collage art. Invite students to define the word collage. "What materials are used to make a collage?" Must a collage always be two-dimensional? Demonstrate how to color black and white photocopied imagery from magazines.

Process
Create Rosa's Bus

1. Model a replica of a 1955-era Montgomery, Alabama, city bus using Model Magic. Set it aside to dry.
2. Use watercolor pencils and watercolor paints to decorate the bus form exterior, and allow the work to dry.

Design the 3-D Collage Timeline

1. Cut out and color photocopied images related to African American experiences that depict people, places, and things from slavery through today using colored pencils.
2. Glue construction paper sheets to corrugated cardboard rectangles. Position two cardboard shapes together on which to construct timeline.
3. Model a road-like timeline surrounded by two- and three-dimensional forms and shapes, sequenced so the articles reflect the Rosa Parks bus ride and key historical events from black American history.

Assessment
Ask students to check the chronological accuracy of civil rights events depicted in the interactive time line. Summarize learning.

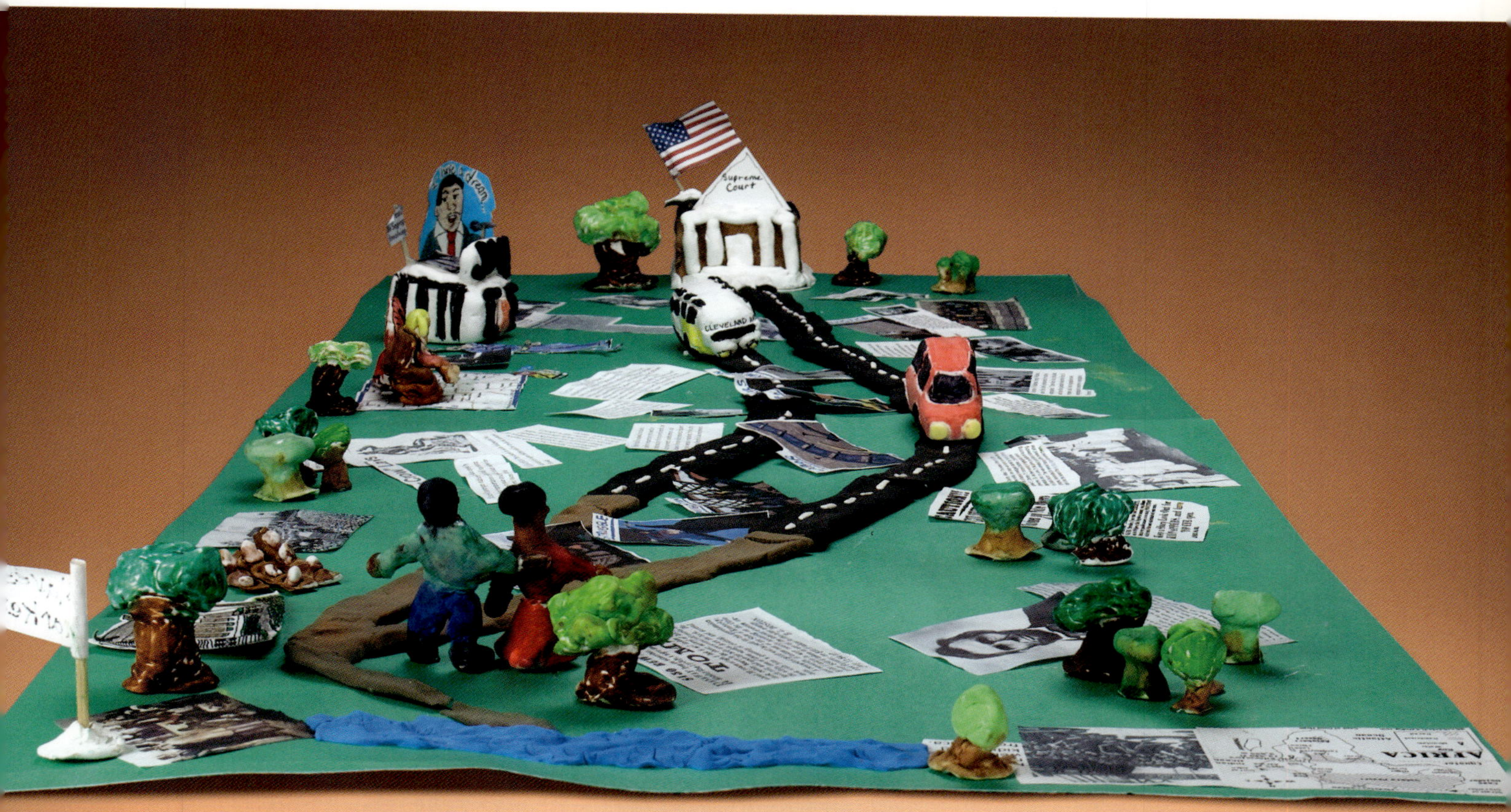

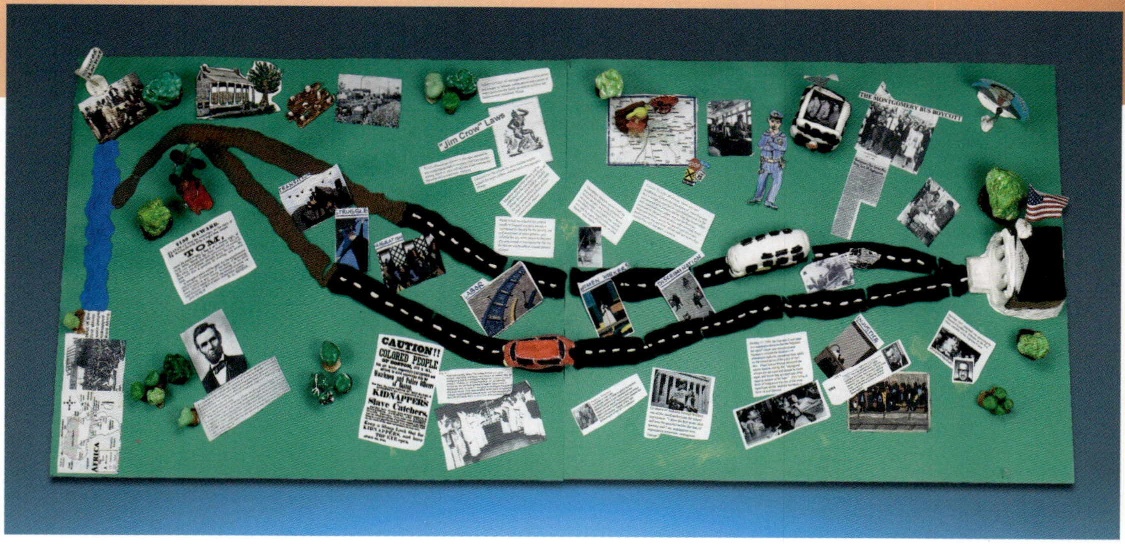

Artwork by students from College Oaks Elementary School, Lake Charles, Louisiana. Teacher: Bobbi Yancey

Background Information

Rosa Parks was a key figure who affected the changes that occurred within the civil rights movement. In 1961, activists and supporters of civil rights decided to take action. Realizing that segregation on interstate buses was unconstitutional, activists organized Freedom Riders to travel throughout the South on buses in an effort to force the Kennedy administration to support the civil rights movement and end segregation. The violence these activists met did not deter them from their work. Finally, under pressure from Robert Kennedy, the Interstate Commerce Commission ruled to outlaw segregation on the interstate buses.

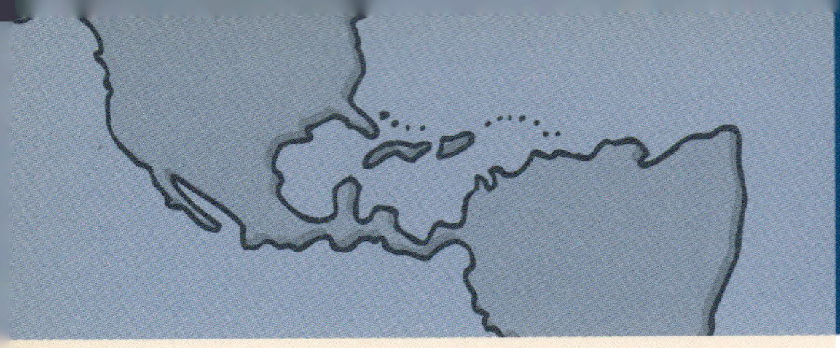

Protecting An Idea

Grade Level
5-6

Classroom Time
Two 40-min. periods

Materials/Tools
- Craft materials
- Crayola® Erasable Colored Pencils
- Crayola Model Magic®
- Crayola Scissors
- Recycled boxes and other items
- White paper

Tips
Use cut plastic coffee stirrers, small recycled boxes, or other items as armatures. Coat the finished miniature invention with a glaze of school glue for added support and strength.

Resources
Alexander Graham Bell by Leonard Everett Fisher
Inventing the Future: A Photobiography of Thomas Alva Edison by Marfe Ferguson Delano
The Smithsonian Book of Flight for Young People by Walter Boyne

Visual Arts Standard 1
Understanding and applying media, techniques, and processes.

Social Studies Standard IIX
Science, Technology, and Society

Objective
Students explore the patent process and then create a miniature model of an invention with a description of how it will benefit society.

Teacher Preparation
Classroom Teacher: Start a display called "Protect Your Invention." Ask students to identify inventions that they see as valuable and find information about the inventors. Ask them to research how ideas and inventions are protected and patented in the United States.

Art Teacher: Display illustrations or photographs of major inventions and the inventors who have helped society through their creative thinking, such as Leondardo da Vinci. Show the development of an invention such as the sewing machine.

Discussion Starters
Classroom Teacher: "What are some inventions that could change the world the way electricity or the telephone did?" "What kinds of ideas can be patented? Imagine an invention You may be on to something big!" Discuss how science and technology enable change. List inventions that are helpful (or harmful) to society.

Art Teacher: "What kinds of things do you like to sketch or scribble? Think about an idea or invention that will help the world and how you might draw it." Show reproductions of the invention sketches that Leonardo da Vinci created.

Process
1. Imagine a new invention that will help the world. What would it do? What would it look like? What technology would it use? What is new about the invention?
2. Sketch your ideas on paper using erasable colored pencils. Erase and make adjustments to your sketch as your ideas become more concrete.
3. Create a miniature model of your invention with Model Magic. Use recycled items for an armature. When it's fresh from the pack, Model Magic sticks to itself and you can embed items in it. Attach other recycled or craft materials to bring your invention to life.
4. Describe to classmates how your invention will benefit society.

Assessment
Exchange sketches, writings, and models with classmates. Discuss why each one would benefit society. Compare and contrast similar inventions. Summarize learning.

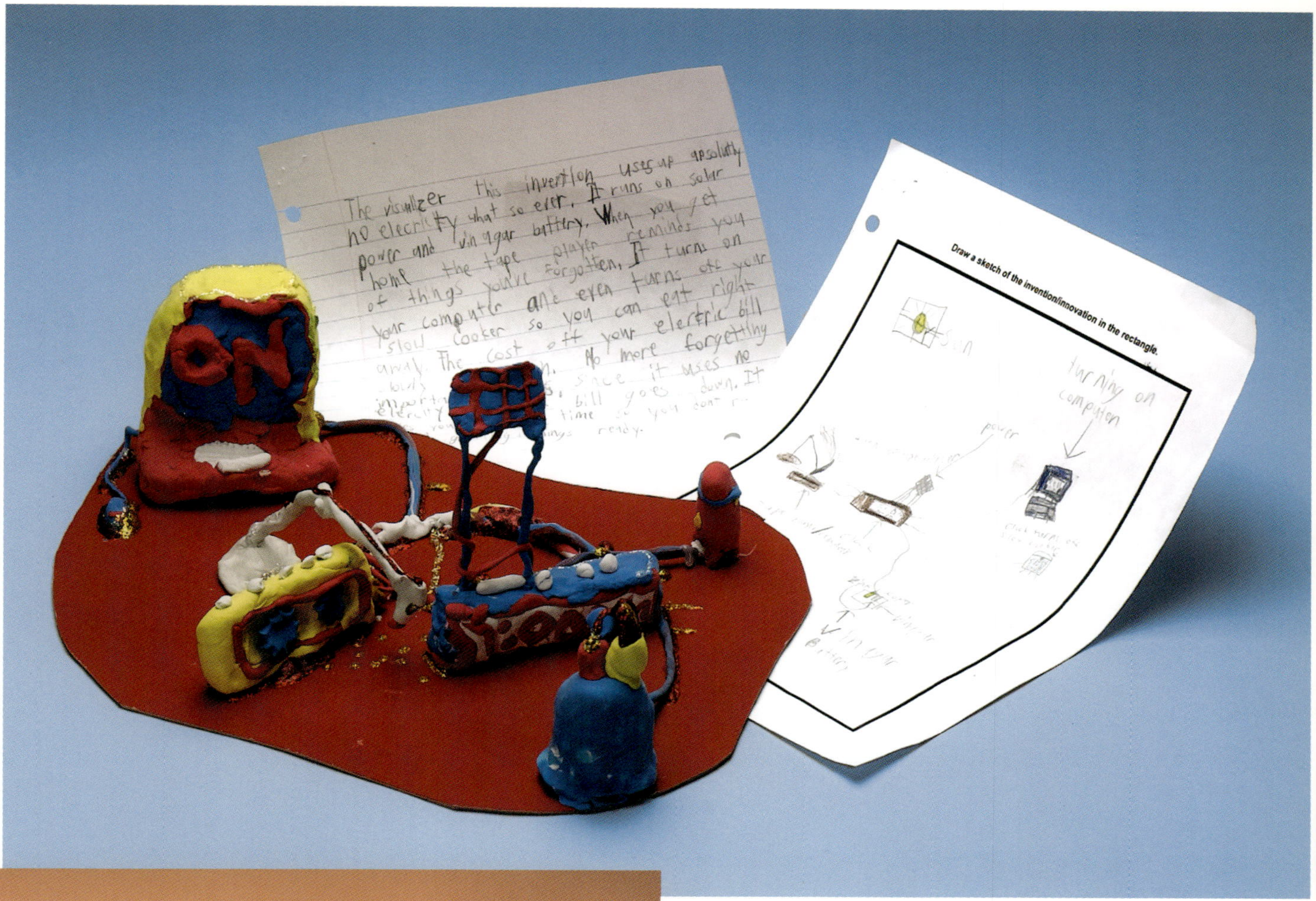

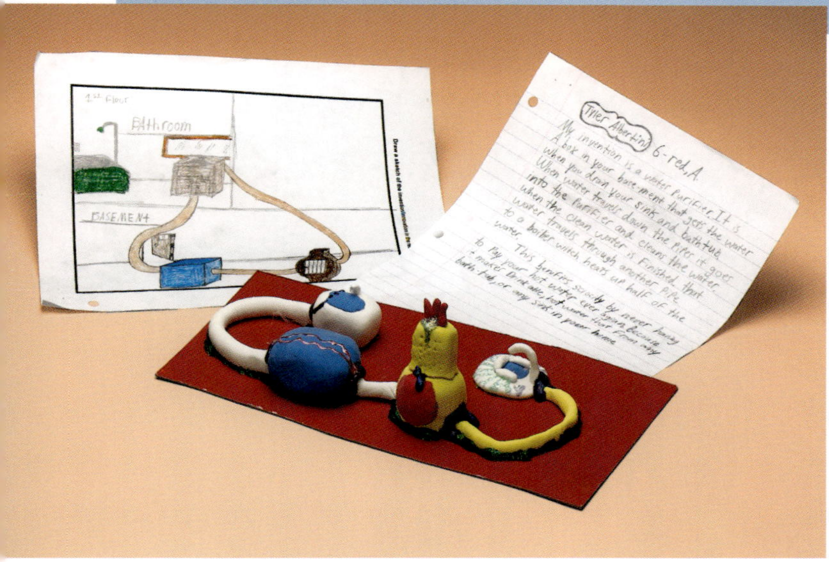

Artwork by students from Maple Avenue Middle School, Littlestown, Pennsylvania. Teacher: Pam Gall

Background Information

Technology can help people invent. Technology also holds hope for a better tomorrow. Every day new cures are being discovered, more efficient forms of electricity are being used, and technology is advancing to make our lives and the lives of future generations better. A patent for an invention is a grant of property right by the U.S. Government to the inventor (or heirs or assigns), acting through the U.S. Patent and Trademark Office. The right granted by the patent is, in the language of the statute, "the right to exclude others from making, using or selling" the invention.

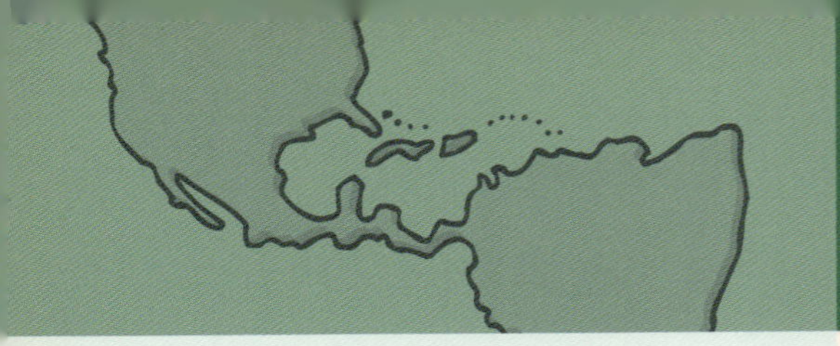

A Forest of Family Trees

See lesson on page 10

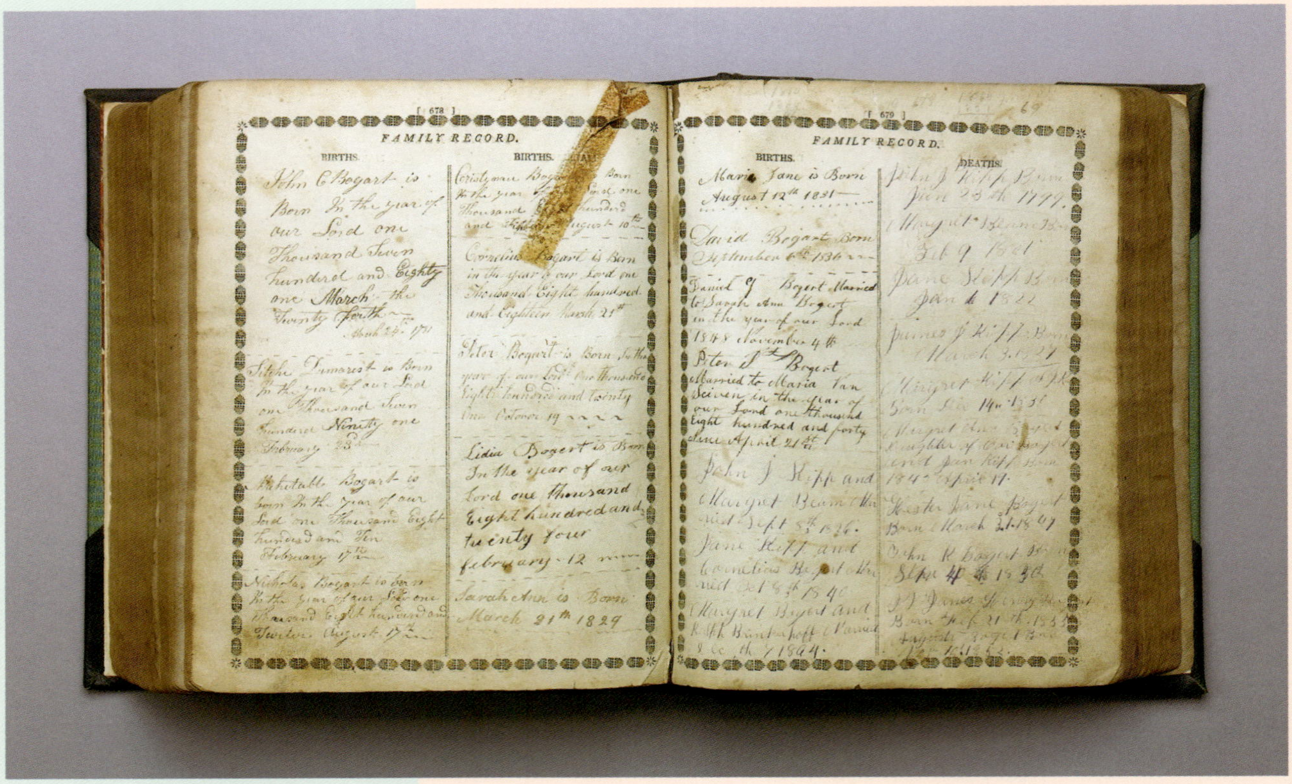

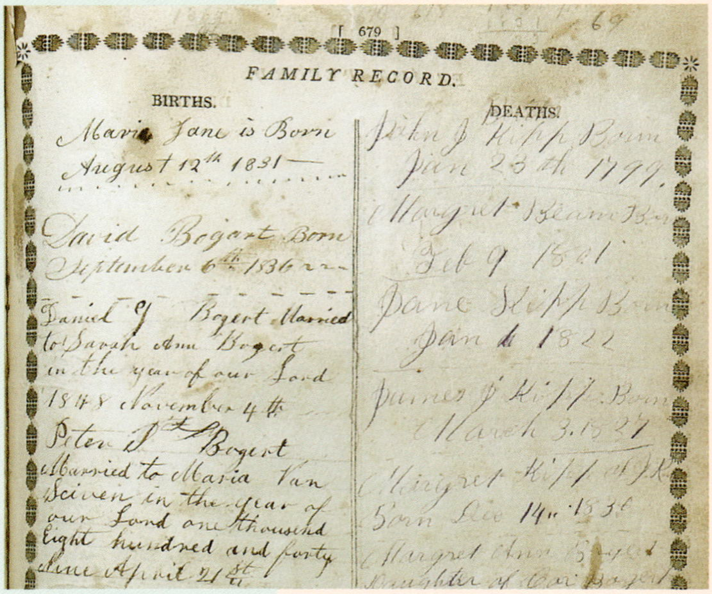

Bogart Family Bible History
Circa 1648
Printed paper
10 1/2" x 16"
Collection of Randy Granger

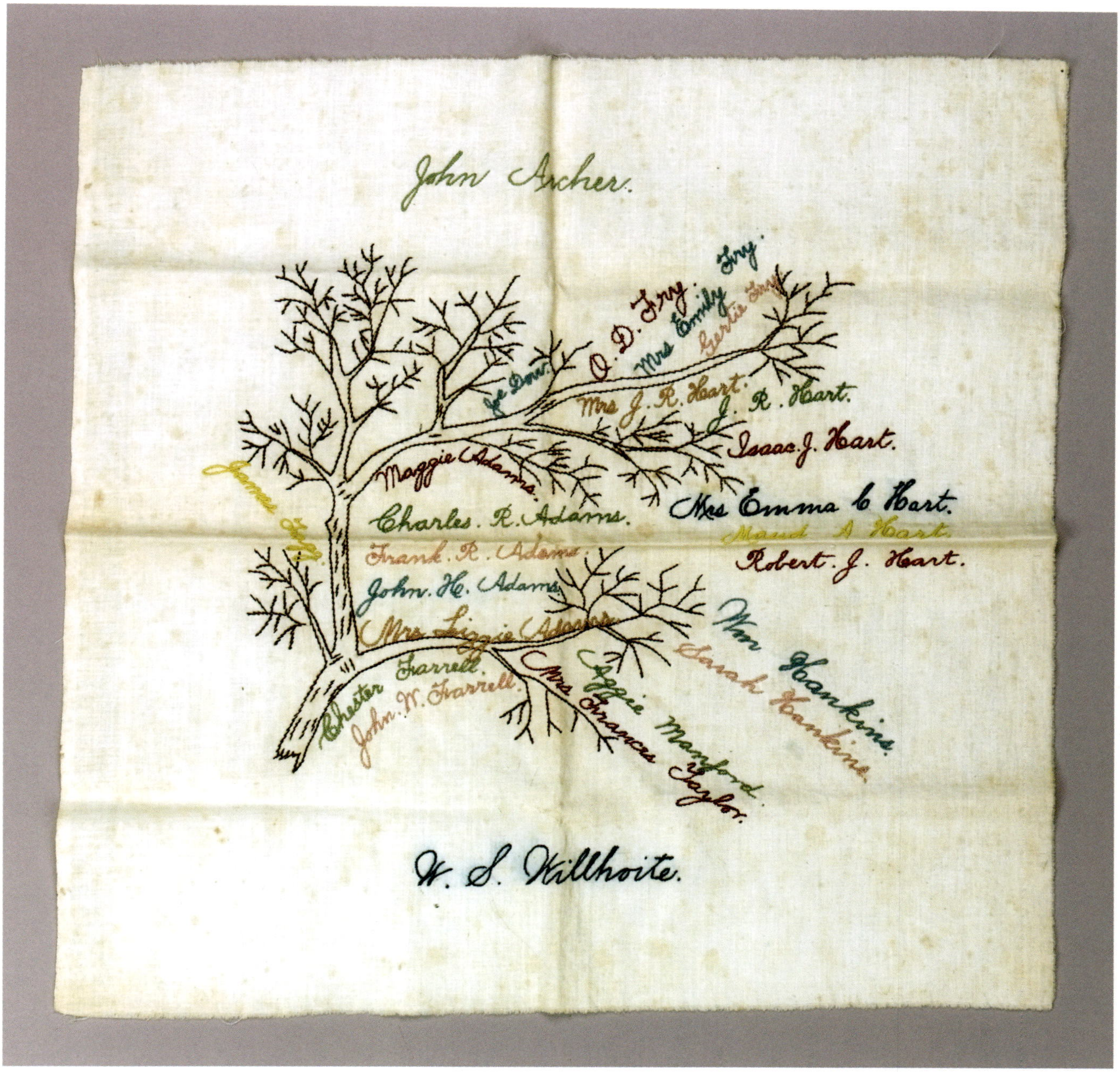

Ruth Adams Family Tree
Circa, 1900
Artist unknown
Needlework on cotton
The Boyer/Adams Collection
Historic Bethlehem Partnerships, Inc.
Bethlehem, Pennsylvania

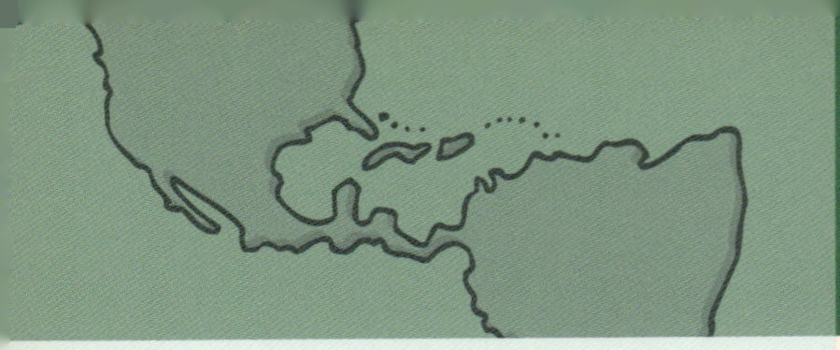

A Forest of Family Trees

See lesson on page 10

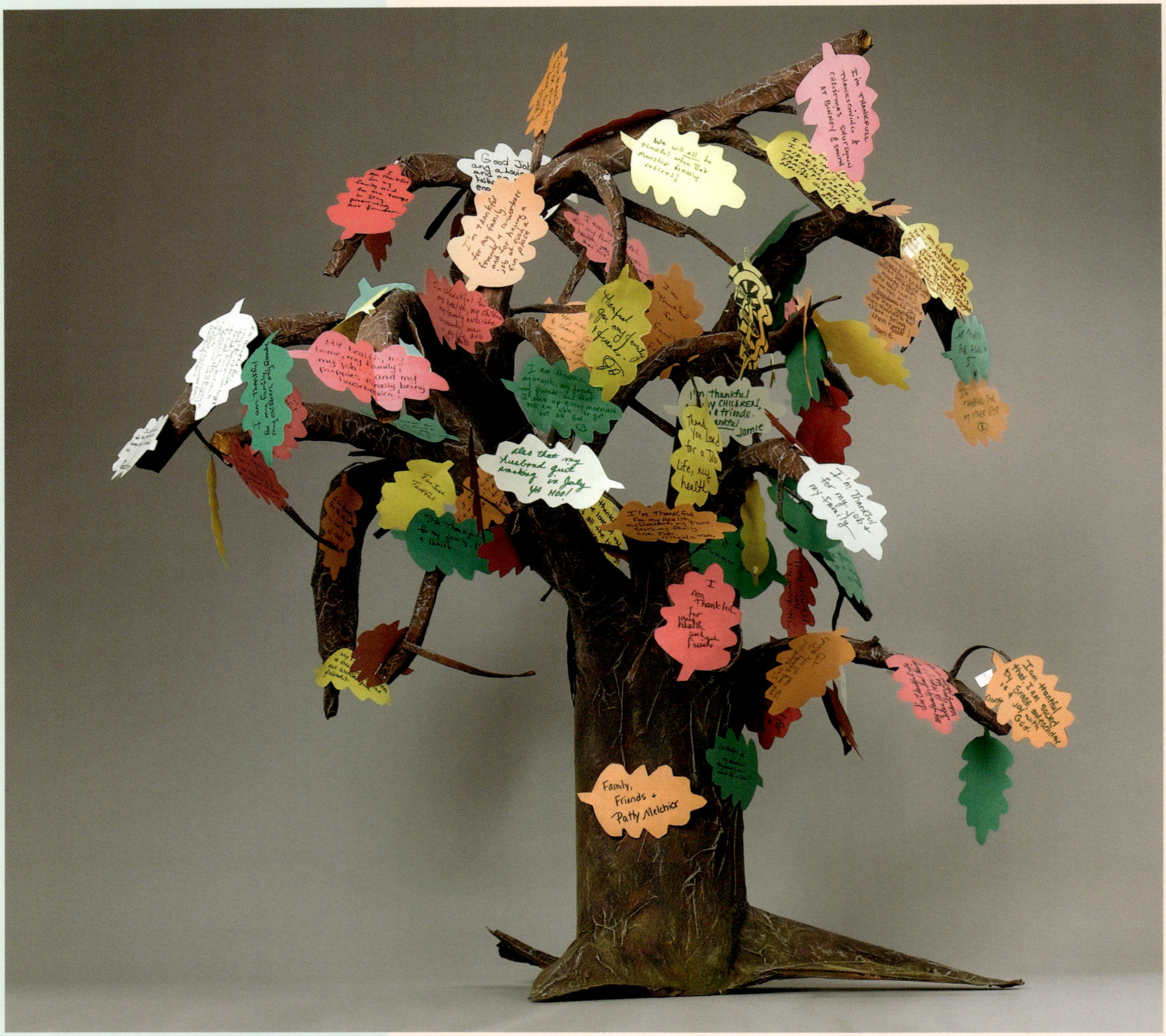

The Thankful Tree
2004
Artists: Margie Bell, Tina Butterfield, Donna Allision, Melissa Moser
Paper maché, paint, cardboard, glue, and construction paper
3' x 3' x 3'
Easton, Pennsylvania
Collection of Binney & Smith, Inc.

Map Your Space

See lesson on page 16

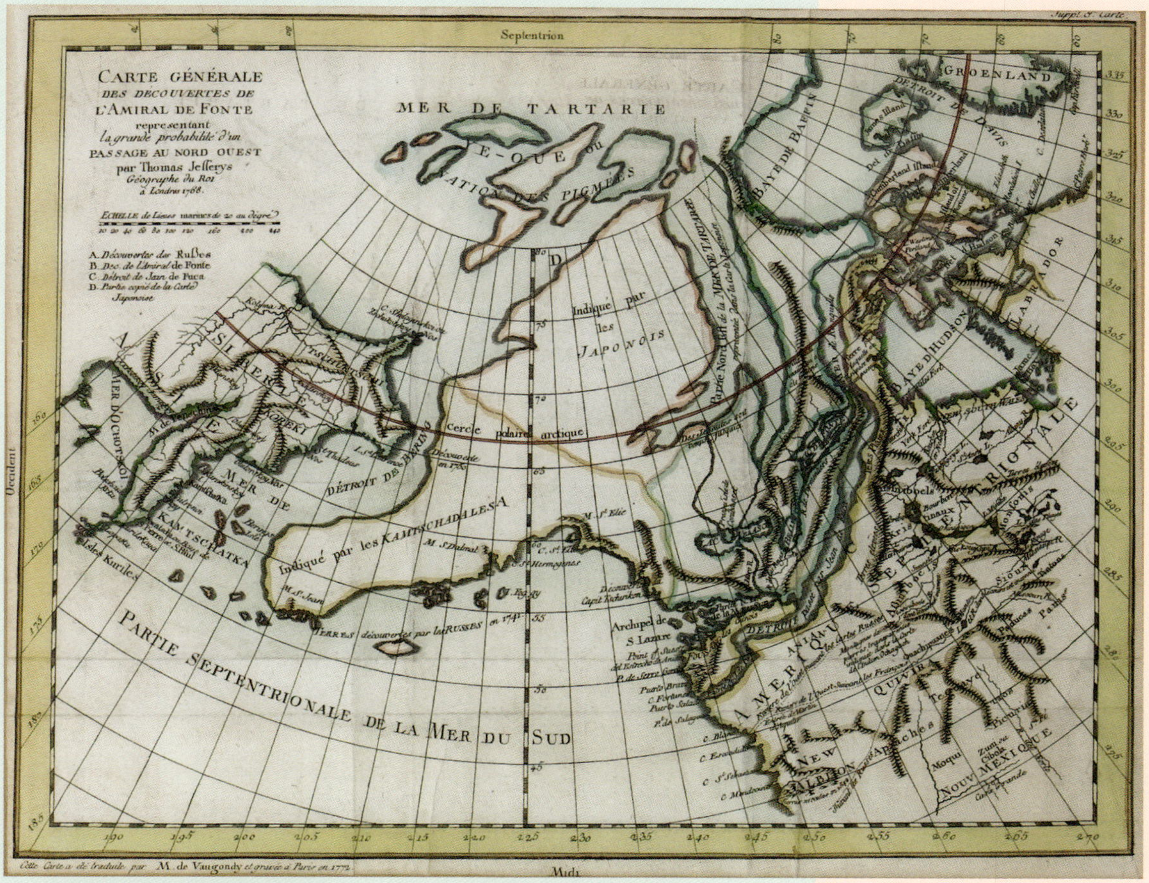

General Map of the Discoveries of Admiral de Fonte
Showing the High Possibility of a Passage to the North West
1772
Artist: Thomas Jefferys
27cm x 34 cm
Paris, France
From the Collection of Barry Goldin

Map Your Space

See lesson on page 16

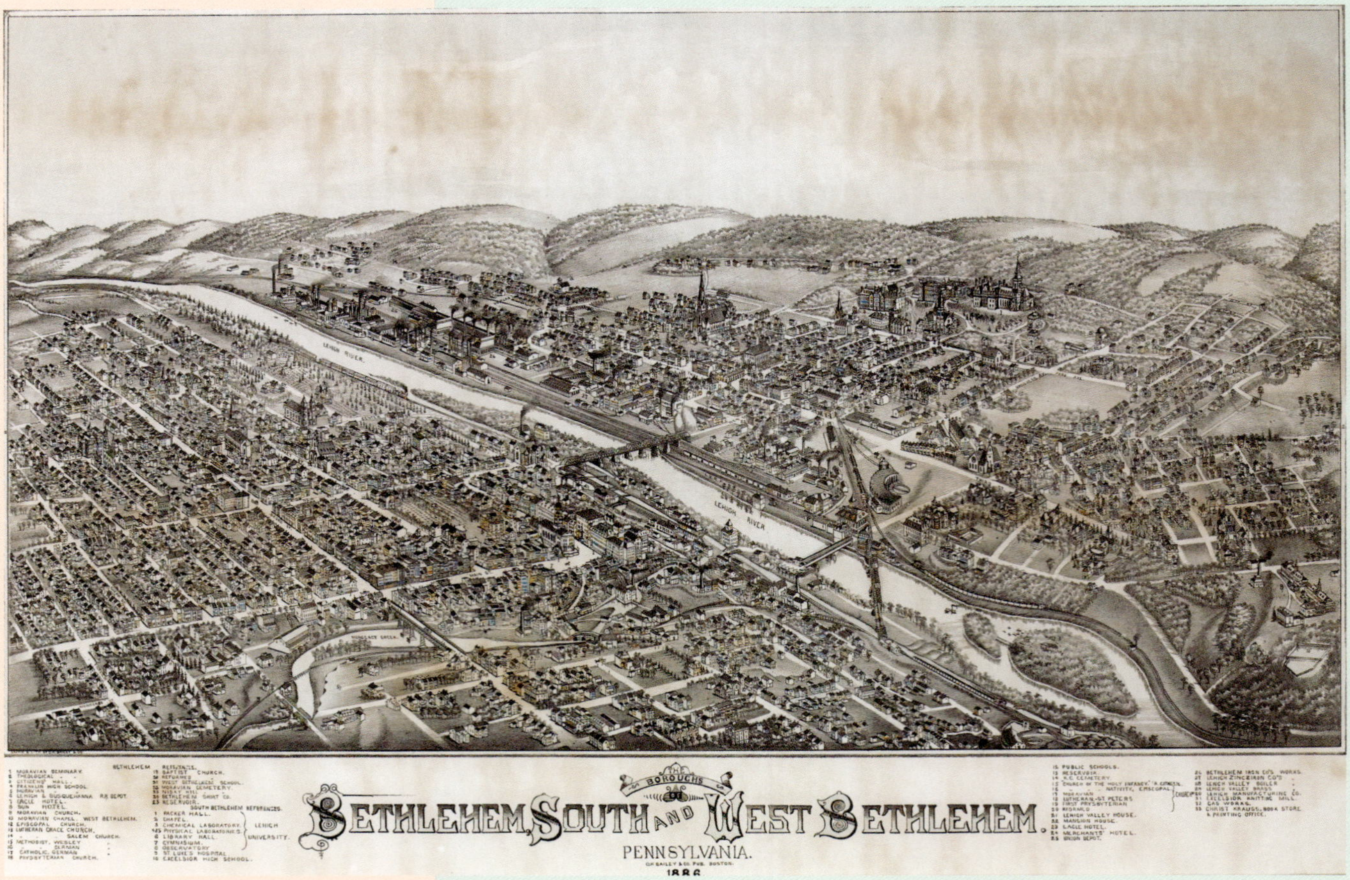

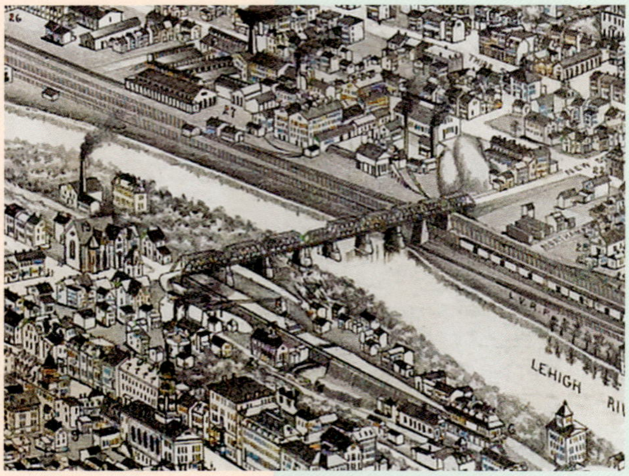

Boroughs of Bethlehem South and West Bethlehem, Pennsylvania
1886
Artist unknown
Printed birds-eye-view map
24" x 42"
Bethlehem, Pennsylvania
From the Collection of Historic Bethlehem Partnership, Inc.

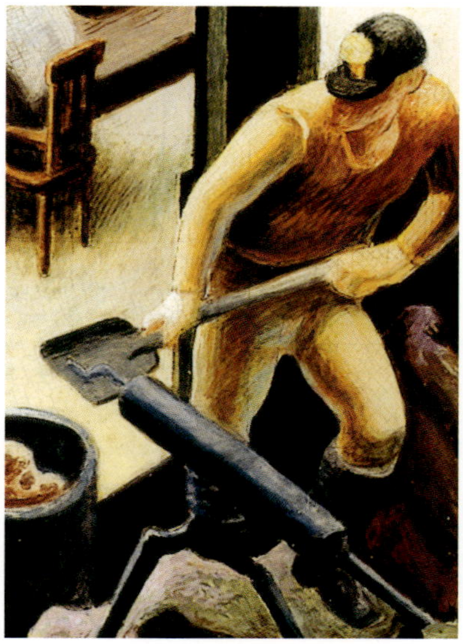

Interior of a Farm House
1936
Artist: Thomas Hart Benton, American, 1889-1975
Tempera on board
18" x 30", SN950
Museum Purchase, Collection of The John and
Mable Ringling Museum of Art,
State Art Museum of Florida

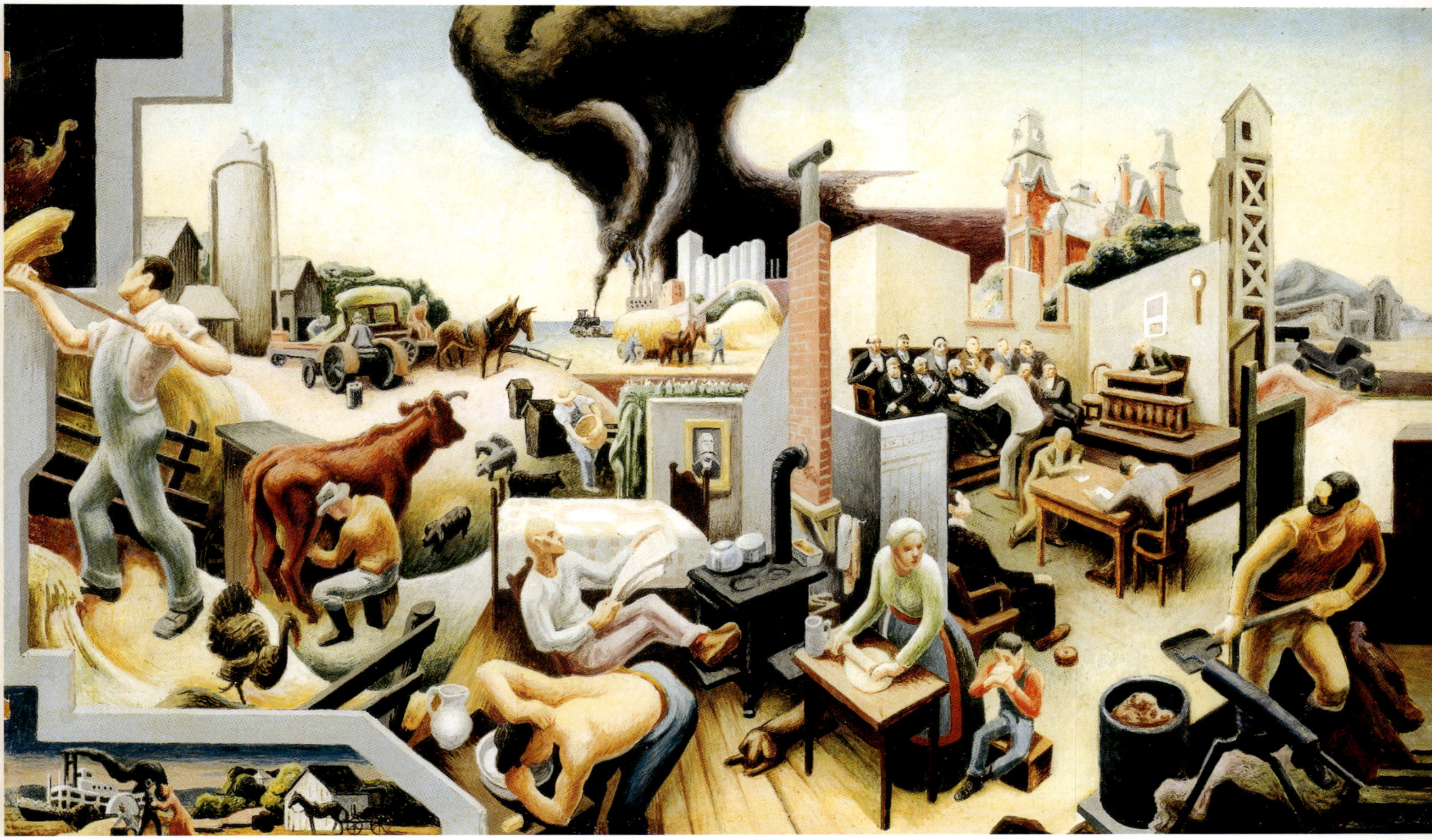

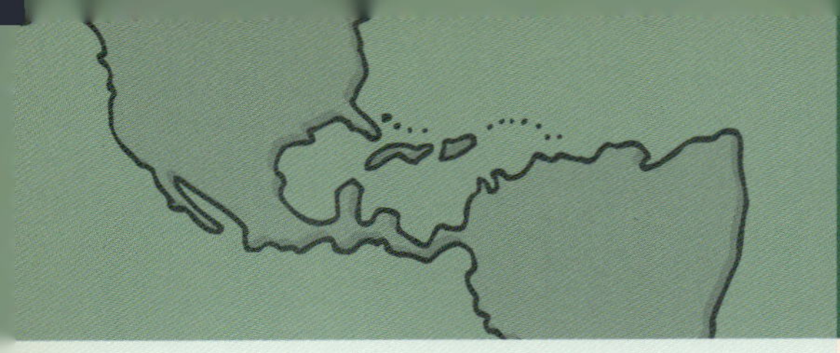

Designing Diversity Dolls

See lesson on page 14

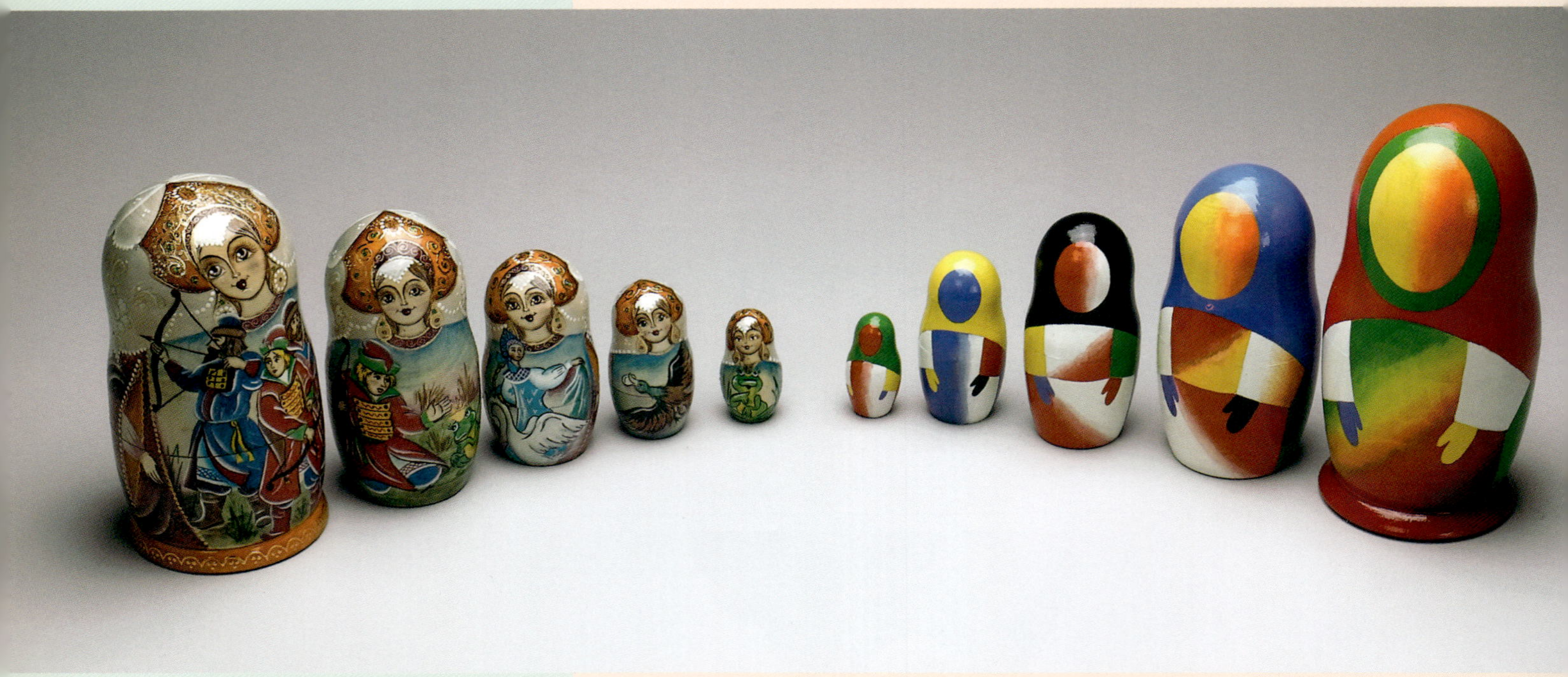

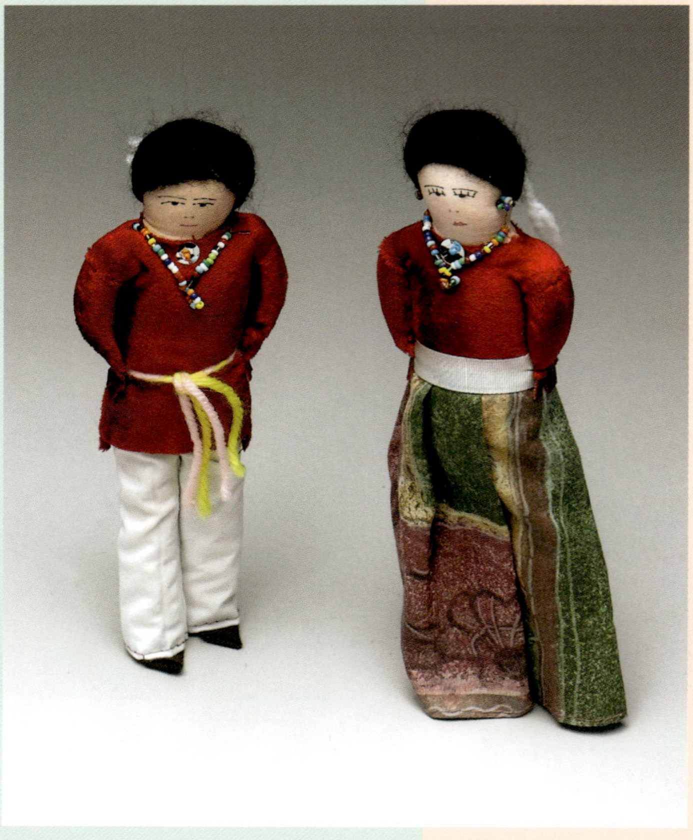

Matryoshka Dolls
Above Left, ***Fairytale Matryoshkas***
2004
Artist unknown
Turned wood, paint, gold leaf
6 1/2" x 3 1/4" x 3 1/4"
St. Petersburg, Russia
Private Collection

Above Right, Kandinsky-like Matryoshka Dolls
2004
Artist unknown
Turned wood, paint
7 1/2" x 4" x 4"
St. Petersburg, Russia
Private Collection

DINE Navajo Dolls
2003
Artist: Alta Silago
Offcut fabric, beads, ribbon, cotton, threads, sequins
8 1/2" x 2 1/2" x 1 1/2"
New Mexico
Private Collection

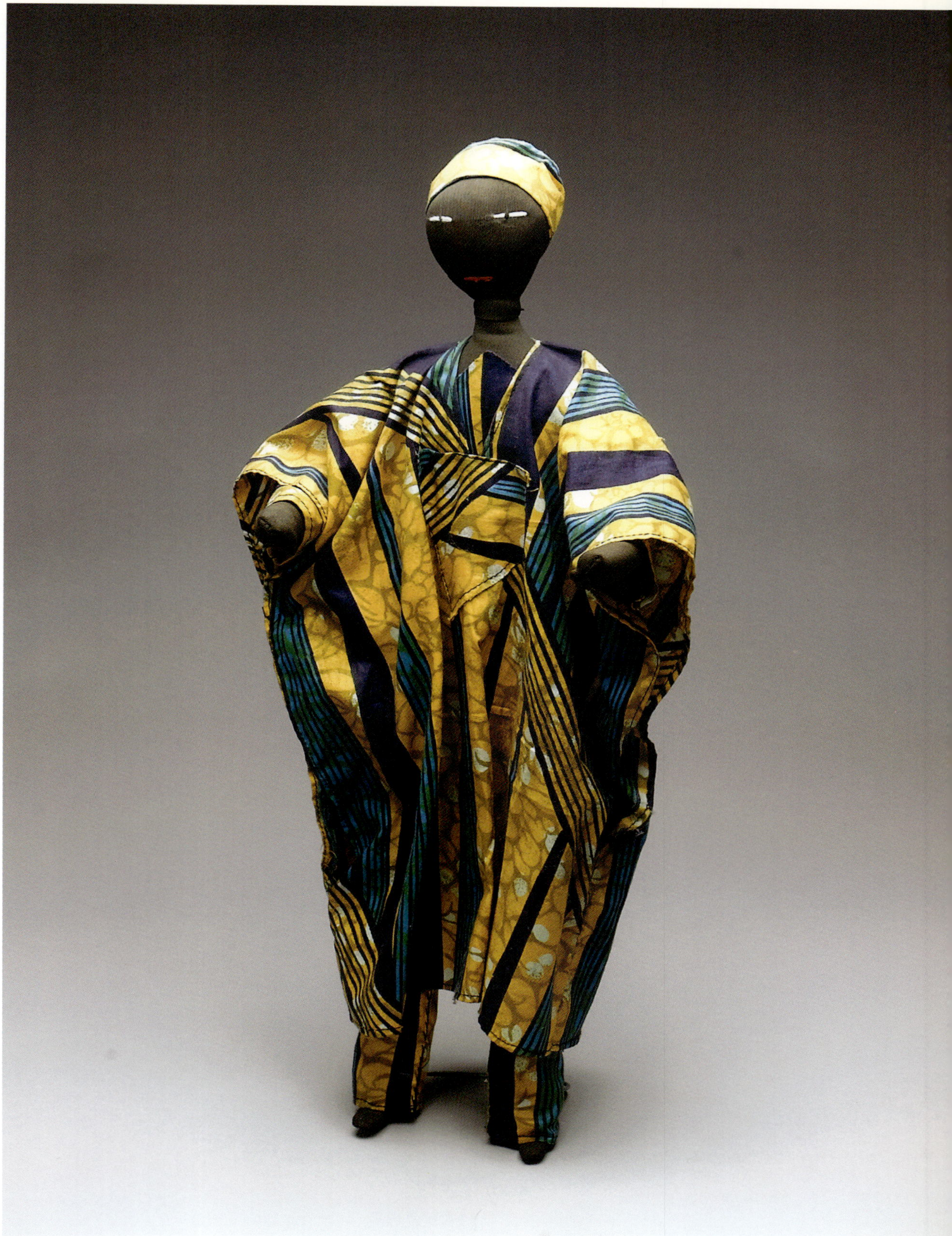

Yoruba Doll
1995
Artist unknown
Cloth, wire, cloth stuffing, thread
10" x 7" x 20"
South West Nigeria, Africa
Private Collection

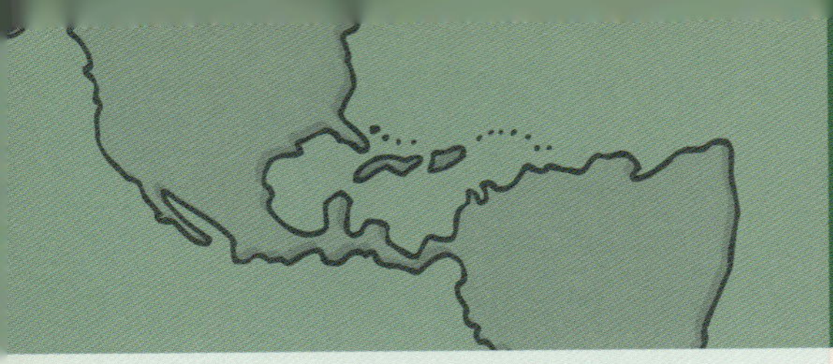

Designing Diversity Dolls

See lesson on page 14

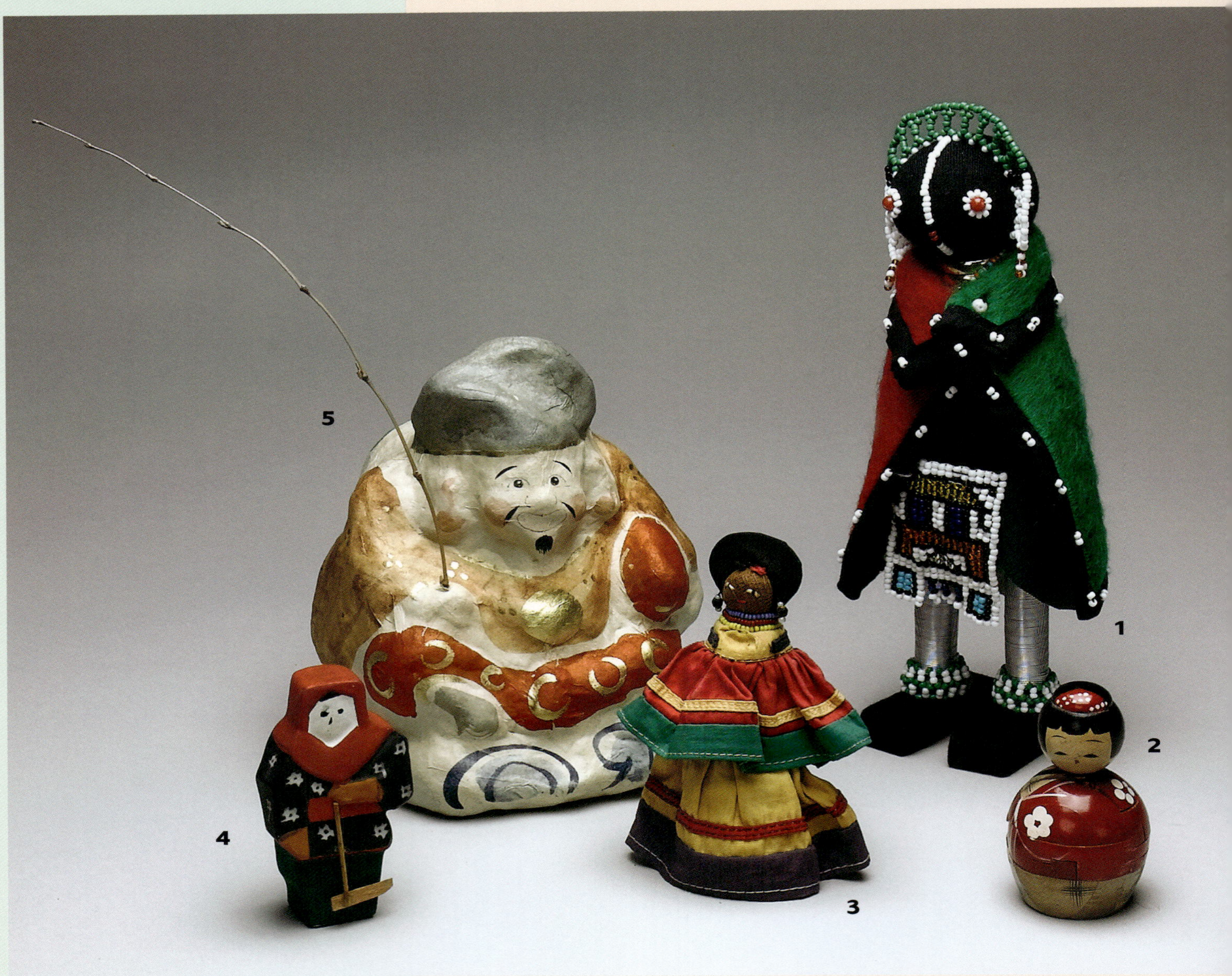

Dolls
Private Collection

1.) African Ndebele Initiation Doll
Artist unknown
Beads, felt, leather, wood and wire
4" x 3 1/2" x 10 1/2"

2.) Japanese Wood Puzzle Doll
Artist unknown
Wood, paint
2" x 2" x 3 1/2"

3.) Seminole Indian Doll
Artist unknown
Beads, cotton fabric, threads, coconut fiber
5 1/4" x 3 1/2" x 1 1/2"

4.) Northwest Alaskan Doll
Artist unknown
Ceramic, metal, paint
2" x 1 1/2" x 3 1/2"

5.) Japanese Paper Mache Doll
Artist unknown
Paper, paint, bamboo, gold leaf
7" x 5 1/2" x 5 1/2"

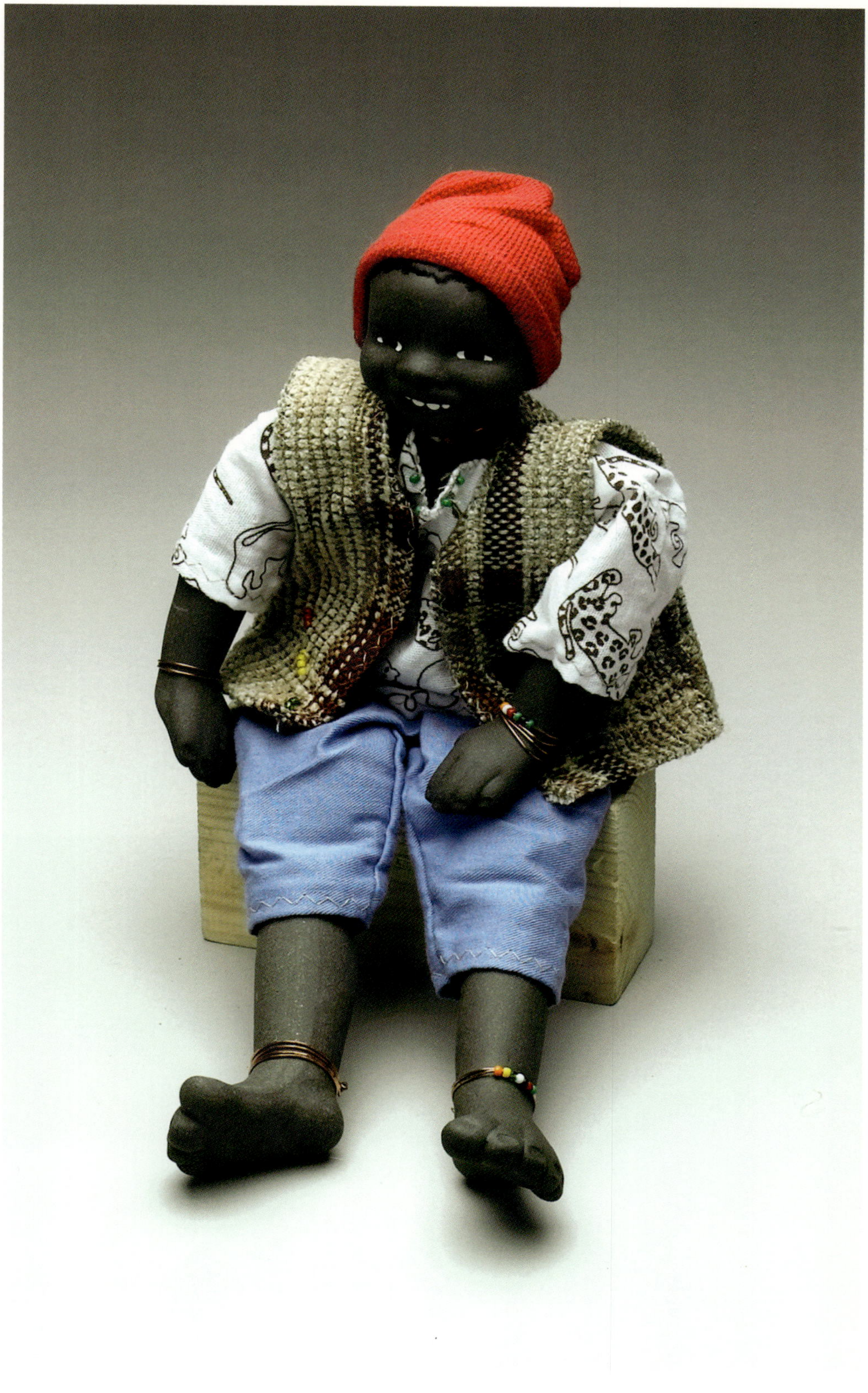

"Bongi" Umntwana Doll
2004
Artist: Carlia de Bruyn
Offcut material, ceramics, paint, beads, wire
12" x 5 1/2" x 2 1/2"
Dressed by Marina
Knysna, South Africa
Private Collection

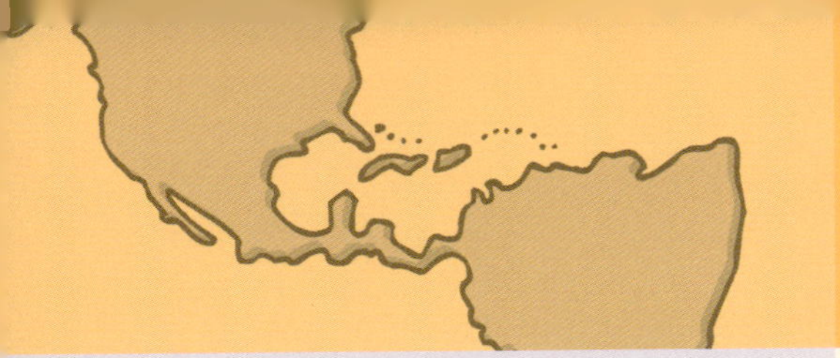

Let's Go Letterbox Hunting

See lesson on page 22

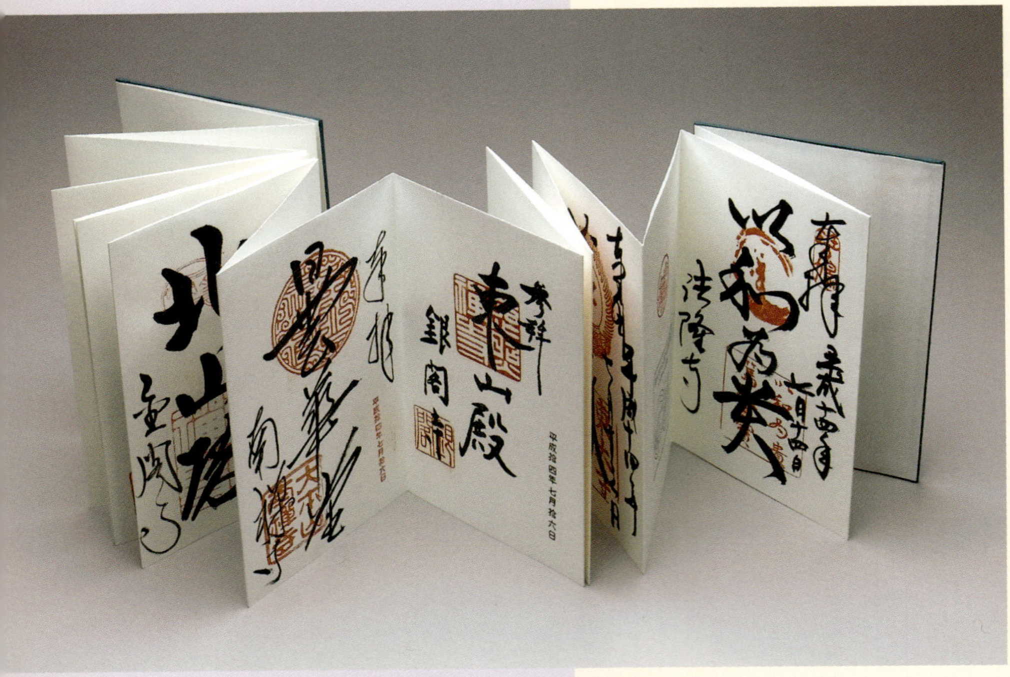

Japanese Temple Stamp Diary
2003
Artist unknown
Paper, silk, ink
4 3/4" x 7 1/8" x 1/2"
Kyoto, Japan
Private Collection

Chops
Private Collection
Left to right:

Chinese Zodiac Rabbit Chop
Carved soapstone
2" x 2" x 4"

Xu Bing Square Word Calligraphy Chop
Carved jade
2 1/4" x 1/2"

Chinese Zodiac Dragon Chop
Carved soapstone
1 1/4" x 1 1/4" x 4"

Griffin Chop
Cast bronze
1 3/8" x 3/8" x 2"

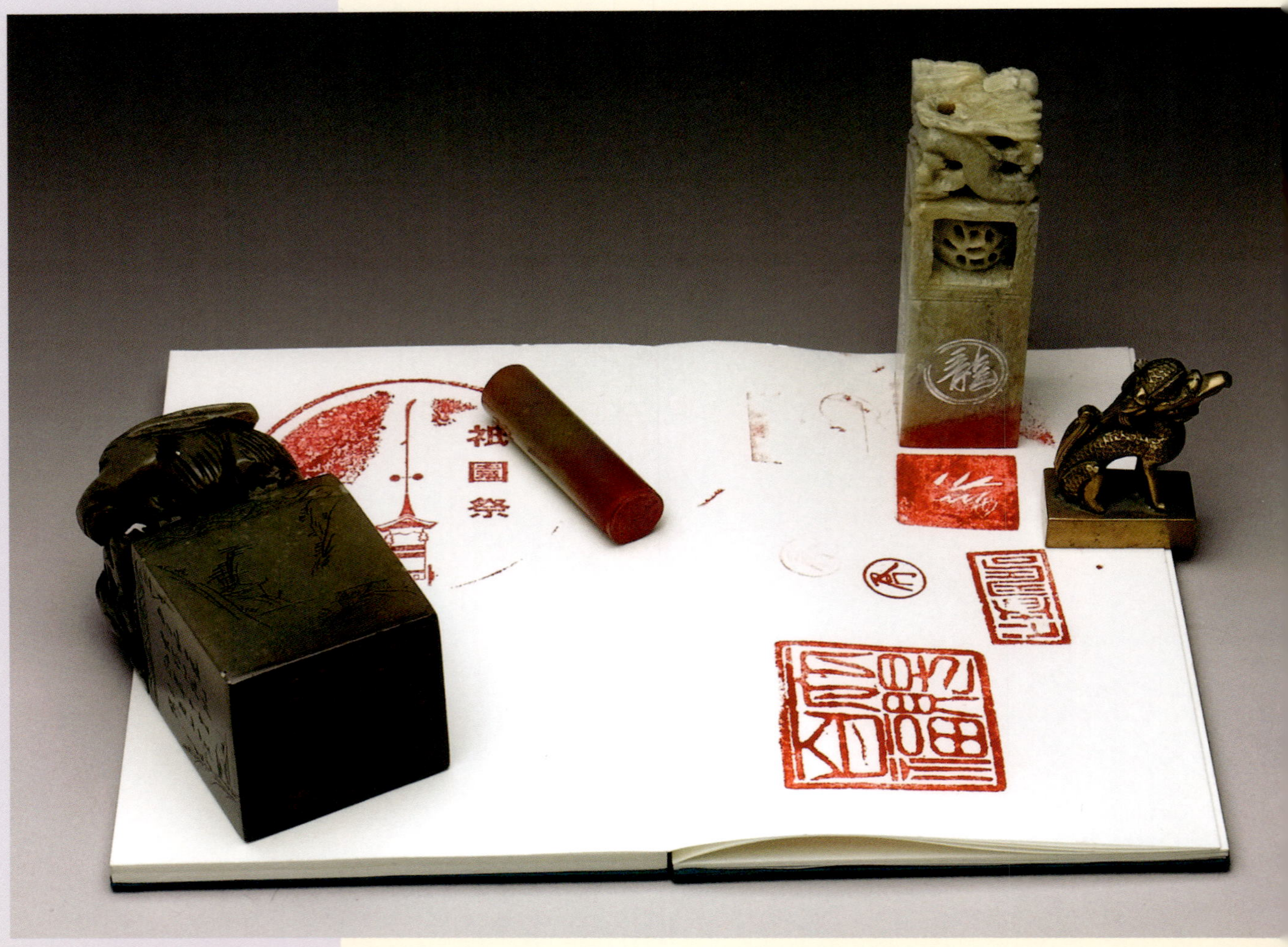

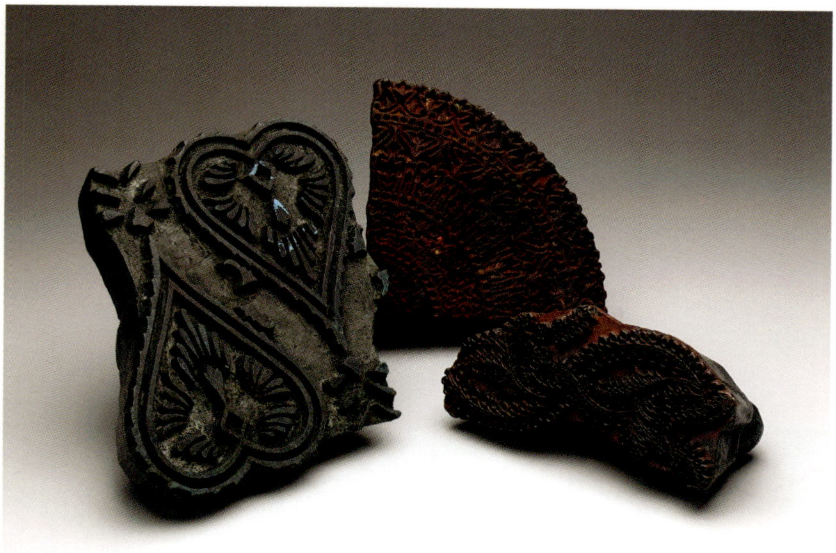

Large Hardwood Batik Stamps
Circa 20th Century
Artist unknown
Carved ebony wood
6" x 6" x 2 1/4"
Indonesia
Private Collection

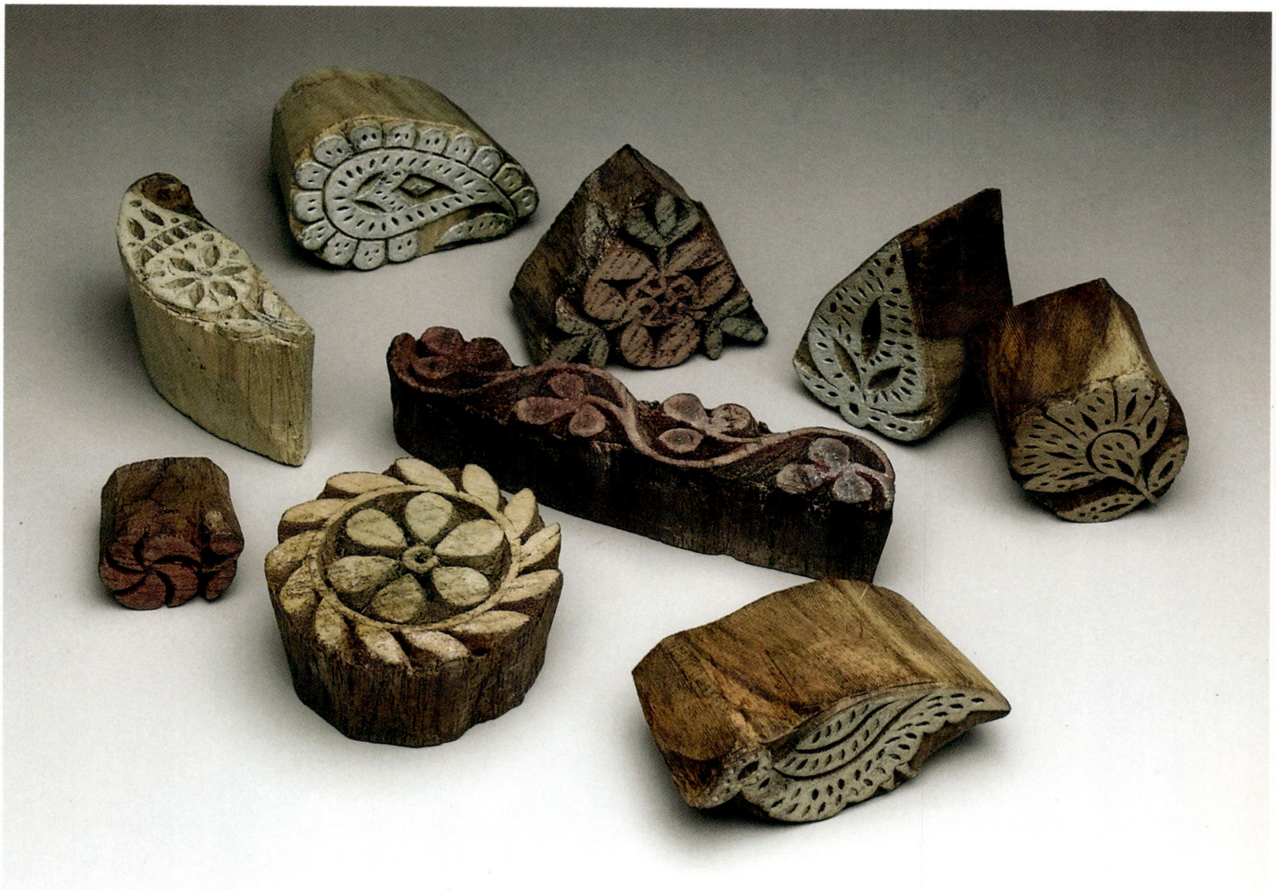

Small Hardwood Batik Stamps
Circa 2000
Artist unknown
Carved hardwoods
Sizes approximately 2" x 2" x 1"
Indonesia
Private Collection

Campaign For Office Of "Leader"

See lesson on page 20

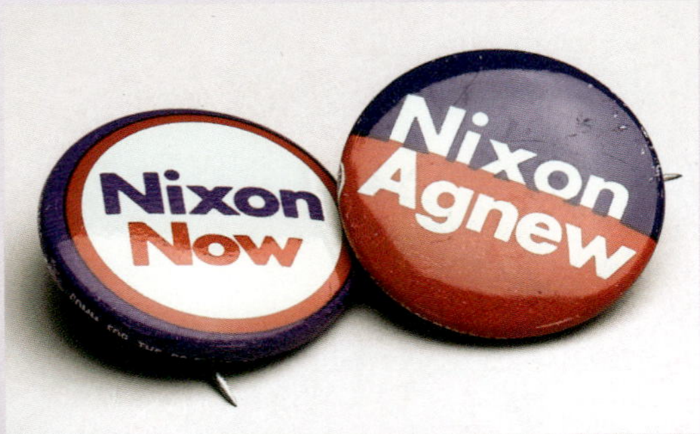

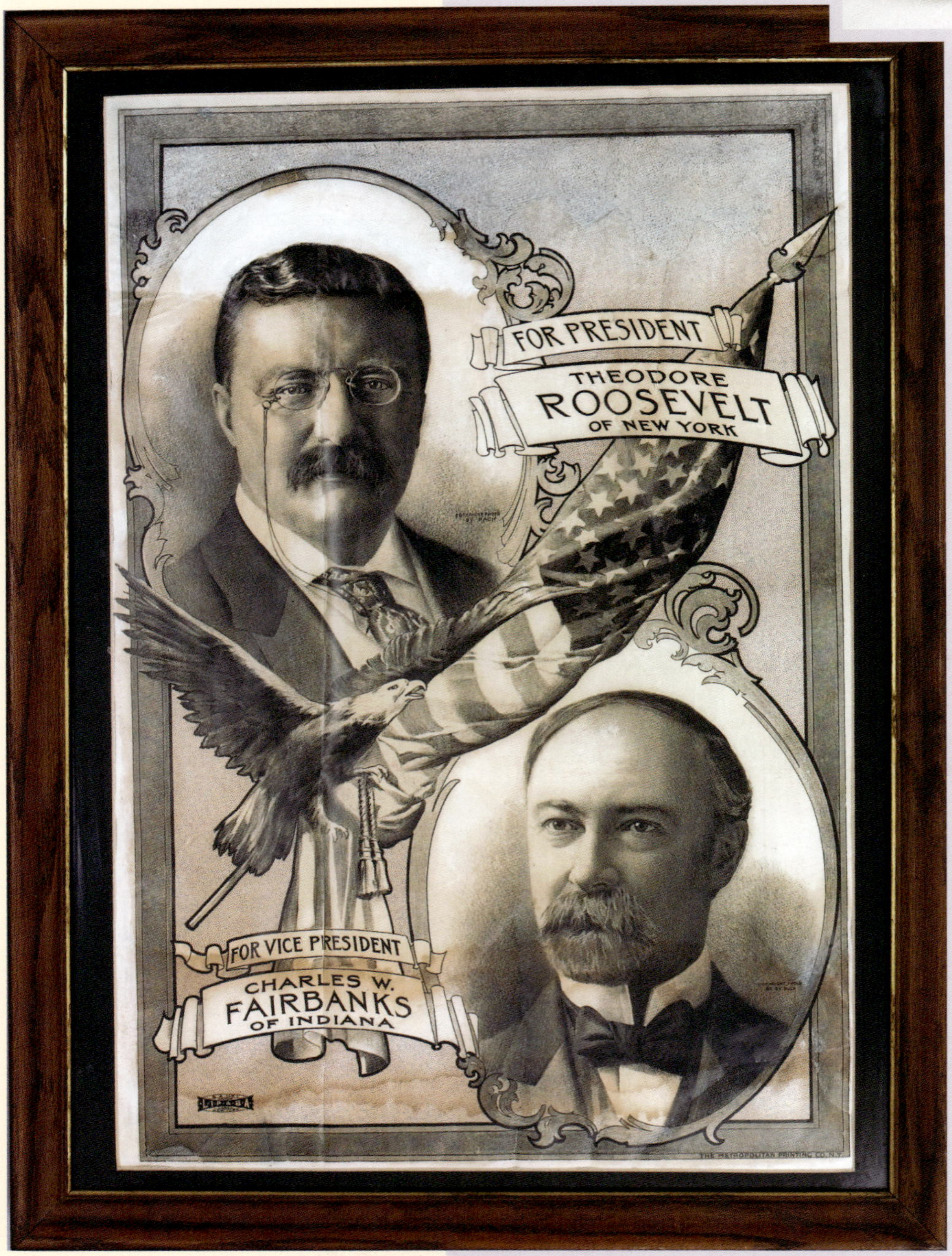

Theodore Roosevelt Campaign Poster
1904
Artist unknown
Colored print reproduction
18" X 24"
Pennsylvania
Collection of Jim Matthews

Richard Nixon Campaign Buttons
1974
Artist unknown
Tin and paint
1" diameter
Pennsylvania
Collection of Ann Lesher